Ann Sta
11.12.15
12/14

# Building Independence

# Building Independence:
## How to Create and Use Structured Work Systems

**Christine E. Reeve, PhD, BCBA-D, and**

**Susan S. Kabot, EdD, CCC-SLP**

**Foreword by Gary Mesibov, PhD**

**Incorporates Evidence-Based Practices**

**AAPC**
**PUBLISHING**

P.O. Box 23173
Shawnee Mission, Kansas 66283-0173
www.aapcpublishing.net

© 2012 AAPC Publishing
P.O. Box 23173
Shawnee Mission, Kansas 66283-0173
www.aapcpublishing.net

Publisher's Cataloging-in-Publication

Reeve, Christine E.

   Building independence : how to create and use structured work systems / Christine E. Reeve, and Susan S. Kabot. -- Shawnee Mission, Kan. : AAPC Publishing, c2012.

      p. ; cm.

      ISBN: 978-1-937473-09-9
      LCCN: 2012942650
      Includes bibliographical references.
      Summary: Detailed description of and rationale for setting up structured work systems for individuals with autism spectrum and related disabilities as a means of fostering independence, skill mastery, reduction of behavioral outbursts, etc.--Publisher.

      1. Autistic children--Education. 2. Children with autism spectrum disorders--Education. 3. Autism spectrum disorders--Patients--Education. 4. Autonomy (Psychology) 5. Learning, Psychology of. 6. Visual learning. 7. Work design. 8. Teachers of children with disabilities--Handbooks, manuals, etc. I. Kabot, Susan. II. Title. III. Title: Structured work systems.

LC4717.8 .R44 2012
371.94--dc23                                                    1207

This book is designed in Sans Culottes and Calibri.

# DEDICATION

Our passion for working with individuals with autism and other developmental disabilities came from personal experiences. As such, we recognize that autism is truly a family affair.

Christine would like to dedicate this book to her sister Mary Ann Reeve. As a special education teacher, Mary Ann daily touches lives of individuals with ASD at work, and at home she does so through her love and support of our sister Cathy and brother-in-law Larry. Without her personal and professional support, this book would not have been possible.

Susan would like to dedicate the book to her sons, John and Brian, for their love and devotion to their brother Michael. Each of you, in your own way has demonstrated your love and commitment to Michael and others with disabilities. I am honored to have raised such caring and thoughtful sons.

# ACKNOWLEDGMENTS

In addition to our families, we would like to acknowledge all of the teachers, administrators, related service providers, and families who have allowed us to take pictures of their classrooms, structured work systems, and tasks. One of the joys that we both find in providing consultation to classrooms and schools throughout the country is that we are able to take ideas from one teacher or classroom and share them with other professionals who may never meet in person. This opportunity to share so many professionals' work with such a wide audience is one of the most rewarding aspects of our jobs.

# FOREWORD

During my almost 40 years of working with people with autism spectrum disorders (ASD) of all ages and levels of functioning, I have studied the many ways that people with ASD think, learn, and understand that are different from those of typical learners and have created some approaches and strategies specifically designed to maximize learning and understanding in individuals who are neurologically atypical. Some of these strategies relate to ways of organizing environments, some relate to developing and organizing materials, and some adjust the ways materials are presented. The overall approach most often associated with my work is called "structured teaching" because many of the strategies that seem most helpful for those with ASD involve structuring the environment, materials, and organizational components of various activities. One of the critical neurological differences between people with ASD and typical learners is that the learners with ASD have problems with structuring their environments, and that is why these approaches are so important.

Of the many aspects of structured teaching, the one I have thought is among the most important is the work system. The work system helps to organize sequences of tasks (e.g., brushing your teeth, washing your face, and combing your hair) and helps people with ASD to take satisfaction in performing these sequences with greater independence, skill, and consistency. Work systems are also motivators because they inform people with ASD in the visual way that helps them understand most clearly exactly what they have to do, how much progress they are making, how much they have left before a positive outcome will occur, and what will happen after the positive outcome. Combining organizational strategies with motivation and the fostering of independence is what makes these work systems so valuable.

Although work systems have been part of the TEACCH structured teaching strategies since the program became statewide in North Carolina in the early 1970s, they seem to have gotten mixed in with the other aspects of structured teaching and never have received the attention they deserve. For this reason, I am delighted to see this book, which finally features work systems and gives many valuable descriptions and examples of exactly what these systems are, how they can be created, strategies for implementation, techniques for collecting data, worksheets that can be helpful while implementing them, and ways that work systems can be used that have been validated as evidence-based practices.

The book has many other appealing features. It is straightforward, concise, clear, and easy to follow. Those working directly with people with ASD will appreciate that jargon is minimized and information is presented with numerous outstanding pictures and creative examples. Inserts are nicely used to supplement major points and expand important concepts. The authors also are very good about presenting numerous options for implementation so that there is no right or wrong way to do things, but a large number of ideas to draw from that help users to understand and implement important priorities and principles.

The book will be most welcome for parents and professionals concerned about people with ASD at all levels of functioning who want a clear description of how to organize sequences of activities to promote skill development and independence. University and continuing education instructors teaching about those with ASD will also benefit from having this book among the required readings. It is a unique book in terms of its comprehensive treatment of the work systems, its concrete, specific, and detailed style, and the many helpful resources, teaching strategies, and suggestions that it offers to those teaching groups as well as individual special educators.

The authors are to be congratulated for presenting such an important intervention technique to those learning about the field or working with those with ASD and doing it with such skill and comprehensiveness.

Gary Mesibov, PhD
*Clinical professor of psychology,*
*University of North Carolina-Chapel Hill,*
*and former director of TEACCH*

# TABLE OF CONTENTS

# STRUCTURED WORK SYSTEMS

*Joey* is a 4-year-old boy who has been diagnosed with an autism spectrum disorder (ASD). He is enrolled in a full-day preschool program designed for children with a variety of special needs. He entered school three months ago and still has significant difficulty working without individual assistance from a staff member. He requires hand-over-hand assistance for most tasks in the classroom, and his teacher has struggled with how to build his ability to work independently. When left to work on his own, Joey often just moves the materials around the area without completing the task. He sometimes gets up and leaves the work area and has to be redirected back.

*Ben* is an 8-year-old boy with autism who spends the majority of his school day in a general education classroom. A paraprofessional in the room supports him as well as several other students. The paraprofessional has to provide Ben a lot of support to keep him on task when the teacher assigns the students work to be completed independently. She has to stand by his desk and redirect him to complete assignments that he should be able to complete on his own. Ben also has difficulty maintaining skills that he has learned and generalizing them from one class to another. He can complete a task in the resource room but struggles to use the same skill in the general education classroom without prompting from the staff.

*Shandra* is an 18-year-old high school student. She spends part of her day in the classroom working on functional academics and part of her day in the community on job sites, rotating through different types of vocational experiences. She is part of a group of students who work at a local hospital receiving support from a job coach. Recently, the job coach has noticed that although the other students are becoming more independent at jobs as they become familiar with them, Shandra still needs someone standing nearby and telling her the sequence of steps needed to complete the work. She sometimes gets part way through a task and then disassembles it.

While individuals on the autism spectrum and related disorders each have unique strengths and weaknesses, many are visual learners who learn best when information is presented in a structured format with a clear beginning and ending point. Structured work systems are designed to take advantage of these strengths to help individuals with ASD learn to complete tasks independently. As such, all of the students above would benefit from the use of structured work systems, originally developed by Treatment and Education of Autistic and related Communication handicapped CHildren (www.teacch.com) at the University of North Carolina at Chapel Hill.

Briefly, structured work systems are designed to give visual information about what work needs to be done, how much work needs to be done, when the work is completed, and what will happen next. The systems use schedules that can involve colors, shapes, numbers, letters, or symbols to indicate what work to do. Schedules can be developed with pieces that can be manipulated (moved around), written on a piece of paper, or on a smart phone or tablet. Work can be contained in baskets, file folders, Trapper Keepers® (loose-leaf binders with multiple folders), or letter trays such as in- and out-boxes. It can be arranged on a desk, on shelves, or on a work table on a job site, depending on the sophistication of the system and the skills of the individual using it. Work is always completed left to right and/or top to bottom. Students never disassemble or reassemble their work when it is completed; instead, each of the completed tasks and the containers used with them are placed in a "finished" basket or area. The number of baskets or tasks depends on the skills of the learner, as does the amount of work placed in each basket.

Some researchers and professionals writing about structured work systems have made a distinction between an activity schedule and the mechanism for telling the student what work needs to be done. These individuals suggest that *schedules identify the location – where the student is to go – whereas the task list indicates what work needs to be done when he or she gets there* (Carnahan, Harte, Schumacher, Hume, & Borders, 2011; Hume & Reynolds, 2010). Other researchers investigating the efficacy of work systems refer to the use of the task list as a schedule (Bennett, Reichow, & Wolery, 2011).

In other areas, activity schedules have been used to refer to schedules that give information both about where the individual should go and the work that needs to be done or the steps in a task (Autism Internet Module, n.d.). In addition, part of the evidence base for work systems has its roots in the research surrounding the use of activity schedules in a variety of forms (e.g., MacDuff, Krantz, & McClannahan, 1993). As such, throughout this book, the writers will refer to the list of tasks to be completed, whether it is shapes to match to baskets or a written list, as a *schedule* or *a work schedule*.

Following are some examples of structured work systems showing varying degrees of sophistication matched to the needs of the individual using them – in this case, Joey, Ben, and Shandra.

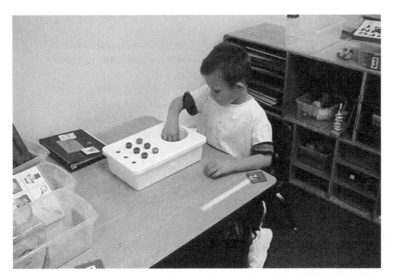

*I1. Joey is completing the last basket In his system. The Velcro® strip on the table to his left held his schedule; it now holds only one visual indicating the reinforcer for completing his work. His communication system is at his right (the blue binder). The task is a simple Shoebox Task® from Centering on Children (www.shoeboxtasks. com).*

*I2. This system was designed for Ben to use in the general education classroom. Ben completes each folder in the letter holder from front to back. When he finishes the task in the folder, he puts the folder on the teacher's desk in an in-box. This also gives him the opportunity to stretch his legs. The divider around his desk keeps him from being distracted by the other students working in the room.*

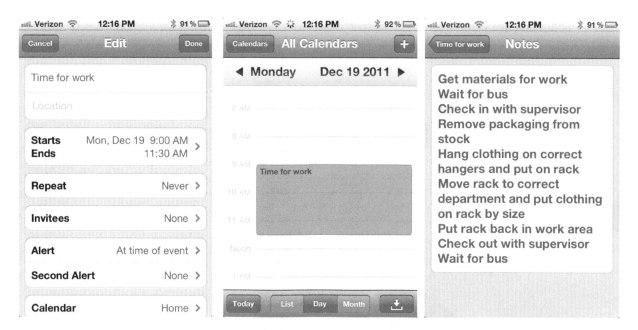

13. Shandra's work schedule is kept on her iPhone calendar app. The first picture shows setting up the worktime calendar, which also has a reminder set to go off at 9 when she is supposed to be at work. The next picture shows the event on the calendar (Time for Work), and the final picture shows the notes that appear with the list of tasks for the work to be completed that appear when she touches the event on the calendar. (For an example in which the student can check off each item as it is completed, the reader is referred to the picture with the Reminders app in the section on schedules, page 31.)

## The Benefits of Structured Work Systems

Structured work systems provide a variety of benefits to individuals with ASD and related disorders. In addition, they offer benefits to classroom, job site, home, and community settings by fostering independence. The following chart lists some of these benefits.

| To the individual | • Promote independence<br>• Build fluency<br>• Maintain previously mastered skills<br>• Generalize previously mastered skills to new materials<br>• Support positive self-esteem and pride in work completed<br>• Calm by reducing social demands<br>• Develop behavioral regulation<br>• Maintain engagement with tasks when not directly receiving instruction<br>• Teach a life-long system that can be used across environments<br>• Provide structure for introducing new skills with less frustration through sabotage of the system |
|---|---|
| To the classroom | • Allow teacher to work with other students while one or more students are using structured work systems<br>• Actively engage students without teacher instruction, reducing stereotypical and challenging behaviors<br>• Train paraprofessionals or peer mentors to teach and monitor tasks |
| To the job site | • Apply a familiar structure to vocational tasks<br>• Teach systems that ensure completion of vocational tasks<br>• Develop independence on the job site |
| To the home and community | • Provide common structure for a variety of functional routines<br>• Allow parents to set up leisure systems so that individuals can remain occupied during busy times (e.g., dinner time)<br>• Apply a known structure to homework tasks |

*Throughout the book, the authors refer to individuals with autism spectrum disorders and related disabilities. Structured work systems are beneficial for people with a variety of special needs, including ASD. In addition, because parts of the book are geared toward educational settings, the authors will refer to individuals using work systems as students or children if the reference is specific to the age. Otherwise, "students" can include preschoolers through adults with a wide range of learning needs and capabilities. We have included specific information about using work systems in schools because they are most frequently used in educational settings. However, the systems would be useful in group homes, employment settings, and vocational training sites as well as being used by parents with their children or adults at home.*

## Why Are Structured Work Systems Important?

Work systems help individuals to start and complete assigned tasks, practice skills they have previously mastered, generalize skills to new materials and situations, and learn to work without assistance from others.

Individuals with ASD and related disorders have difficulty maintaining and generalizing skills. Through the visual structure of the system, they understand the expectations of the task, the work that needs to be completed, and what to do when the work is finished. Because the system is designed to teach independence, all assignments contained in the system *must be previously mastered tasks*. The work system provides the opportunity to practice a skill in order to maintain and apply it to new materials and situations and, thereby, generalize knowledge.

Many individuals with ASD also have difficulty learning to work by themselves, relying on others to provide prompts and assistance through simple tasks that are performed every day. This tendency toward prompt dependence makes it imperative that teachers and other adults promote independence. Work systems provide clear cues to the individual that he or she is expected to work independently of adults. They should be taught in such a way as to minimize and fade adult assistance for work completion. Because all of the tasks have been previously mastered (see above), it is reasonable to expect the individual to complete the work independently.

For Joey, the work system provides an opportunity to learn to complete a simple task from beginning to end with no adult assistance. Learning to work independently is a critical skill for a child such as Joey, who requires 1:1 assistance and supervision for nearly every activity of his day. For example, learning to complete tasks independently can mean that his teacher can be with another student while he is working, or his parent can cook dinner while giving him a set of tasks to finish.

For Ben, structured work systems provide an opportunity to work without assistance from his paraprofessional in a general education classroom. This supports his independence while also helping him to assimilate with the general education students. In addition, because the system gives him the cues needed to do his work, it provides opportunities for Ben to practice skills in the general education classroom and generalize them between the resource and general education classes without the assistance of adults. Further, this allows the paraprofessional to provide support to more students in the classroom while Ben is working on his own.

Finally, for Shandra, a structured work system may mean the opportunity to continue on a job site with a visual system once the job coach has been faded out. A work system that teaches Shandra where to put her completed work and what comes next will help her to work on a task from beginning to end without reminders. This will greatly increase her employment opportunities in the community because she will need less adult support.

## Evidence Base for Structured Work Systems

*Structured work systems, also known as independent work systems (National Professional Development Center on Autism Spectrum Disorders [NPD], 2008) and structured teaching (National Autism Center, 2009), are recognized as an evidence-based practice by the NPD and as an emerging best practice by the National Autism Center (2009).*

*This recognition is based on studies beginning in the early 1990s with the work of the Princeton Child Development Center on photographic activity schedules (Krantz, MacDuff, & McClannahan, 1993; MacDuff, Krantz, & McClannahan, 1993). Later work focused on using visual supports for transitions (Dettmer, Simpson, Myles, & Ganz, 2000) and structured work systems themselves (Bennett, Reichow, & Wolery, 2011; Hume & Odom, 2007; Hume, Plavnick, & Odom, 2012). Studies have been conducted on preschool, elementary, and middle school-aged children and, therefore, it is reasonable to assume that they can be effective across a wide range of ages and environments.*

## Characteristics of Autism Spectrum and Related Disorders That Dictate the Need for Structured Work Systems (continued)

| Characteristic features of individuals with ASD | Characteristics of Structured Work Systems | | | | | | | |
|---|---|---|---|---|---|---|---|---|
| | Visual schedule | Working top to bottom, left to right | Practicing only mastered tasks, often with new material | Clear indication of work to be done | "Finished" basket or place | What to do next | Non-verbal prompting | Work materials and tasks |
| Expresses strong need for routine or sameness | X | X | | X | X | | | |
| Expresses desire for repetition | X | X | X | | X | | | |
| Has strong need for closure or difficulty stopping a task before its completion | | | | X | X | | | |
| Has difficulty asking for help | | | X | | | X | | |
| Has difficulty following directions | X | X | | | | X | X | |
| Has poor organizational skills | X | X | | X | X | X | | X |
| Has difficulty starting or completing actions; learned helplessness | X | | | | | X | X | |
| Chooses or prefers solitary activities | | | X | | | | X | |

| Characteristic features of individuals with ASD | Visual schedule | Working top to bottom, left to right | Practicing only mastered tasks, often with new material | Clear indication of work to be done | "Finished" basket or place | What to do next | Non-verbal prompting | Work materials and tasks |
|---|---|---|---|---|---|---|---|---|
| Has difficulty applying learned skills in new settings; generalization | | | X | | | | | |
| Recalls information inconsistently; loses skills previously mastered | | | X | | | | | |
| Has low frustration tolerance | X | X | X | X | | X | X | |
| Has difficulty tolerating mistakes | | | X | X | | | | |
| Responds better to visual than auditory directions | X | | | | X | X | X | X |
| Uses objects in an atypical, repetitive manner | X | | | | X | | | X |
| Has difficulty maintaining attention and engaging in meaningful self-directed activities outside their special interest | X | X | X | X | X | X | X | X |
| Does not generalize new skills to new materials and settings | X | | X | | | | | X |

Note. The characteristics listed here represent a partial list from the *Underlying Characteristics Checklist – High-Functioning* and *Underlying Characteristics Checklist – Classic* by Ruth Aspy and Barry G. Grossman and the *Underlying Characteristics Checklist – Early Childhood* by Ruth Aspy, Barry G. Grossman, and Katherine Quill. Available from www.aapcpublishing.net.

# COMPONENTS AND USE OF STRUCTURED WORK SYSTEMS

Work systems are designed to answer four essential questions (Schopler, Mesibov, & Hearsey, 1995), which form the basis of the structure of the system:

1. What work do I need to do?
2. How much work do I need to do?
3. How do I know when I'm finished?
4. What do I do next?

As illustrated in the following, the elements of the system are designed specifically to answer these questions so that students are able to both initiate and complete the tasks assigned without having to request assistance.

## What Work Do I Need to Do?

In order to work independently, we need to know what is expected. Work systems are designed to help focus on what needs to be completed. The tasks that the student is expected to finish are often organized in clear plastic containers or in containers without lids that allow her to see exactly what needs to be done. Sometimes teachers organize work in file folders or Trapper Keepers® that the student has to open to see the items that must be completed. The decision about which format of a system to use is based upon the needs of a given student.

*H1. These two pictures show the use of a Trapper Keeper® or multifolder notebook that has been set up for a work system. The first picture shows the order of the work to be done, with one task or set of tasks in each folder. The second picture shows a picture of the first folder opened – the student completes the work in the "To do" pocket and places it in the "finished" pocket. This system works well for a student who has to take his work system with him to different environments.*

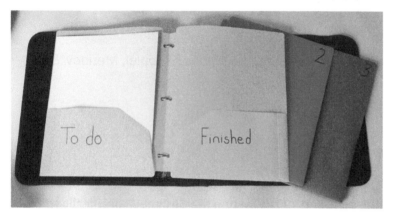

*H2. This middle school teacher chose to stack her baskets to leave more room for the student to work at the table. In this system, the student matches the letter on the schedule (on the left) to the corresponding letter on a basket and completes the task. (The "finished" basket is out of the picture on the floor to the right.) When the student finishes all three baskets, he is reinforced with M&Ms (the last picture on the schedule).*

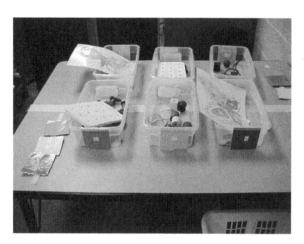

*H3. This setup shows one table being used for two systems, with the table divided by masking tape down the middle. The students sit facing each other to do their work. This setup is handy when there is limited furniture available in the room and the students are not typically distracted by the actions of others working in the vicinity.*

## How Much Work Do I Need to Do?

When using structured work systems, the individual can see how much work he has to do in one of two ways: (a) If he is able to use a visual work schedule (see H4), the number of symbols or the written list will tell him how many tasks to accomplish. (b) If he can't use a visual task list, the number of baskets at his work area will provide the necessary information. For example, if an individual is sitting at his work area and there is one basket in front of him, he is expected to complete just that one task. Another student may be sitting at a work area and have a schedule showing four symbols, each representing a task. He will be expected to complete all four of them.

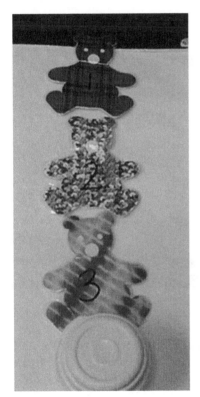

*H4. These bears form a schedule for matching bears on the baskets for a preschool or early elementary system. The plastic container at the bottom of the schedule might contain an edible reinforcer for the child when his work is completed. In this example, the schedule visuals are designed to match a theme in a classroom for young children.*

*H5. Schedules can also list the baskets the student has to get from a shelf. In this system, the student matches the number on his schedule to the number on a basket, brings that basket back to the table, completes it, puts it in a "finished" area or box, and then retrieves the next numbered basket. As can be seen, the numbers in the schedule are not in order. This is done purposely so that students follow the order, not just sequential numbers.*

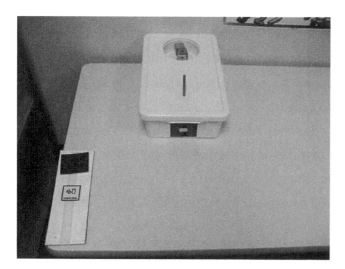

*H6. This is a structured work system with only one basket and a matching symbol. The number of baskets in a system can vary depending on the student's proficiency.*

*H7. In this picture the student is to complete two tasks and place each in the "finished" basket located in the upper-right-hand corner of the table. The clipboard on the right holds visuals of reinforcer choices for when the system is complete. The visual hanging above the table is a place where the student checks in with a matching icon from his full-day schedule.*

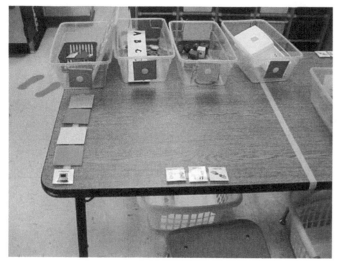

*H8. This is the setup of a structured work system for a self-contained elementary classroom for students with ASD and related disabilities. The students match the colored squares on the schedule to those on the basket and place the basket in the white "finished" basket on the floor to the right. As a reinforcer, this student goes to the computer when his work is completed, as indicated by the picture on the bottom of the schedule. The visuals at the bottom of the table cue the student to communicate for help, a break, or attention.*

Within each work task, only the amount of work expected to be completed is placed in the container. For example, if the student is expected to sort 10 items, only 10 items would be placed in the container in the work system. This way, the student knows what is expected and does not get confused.

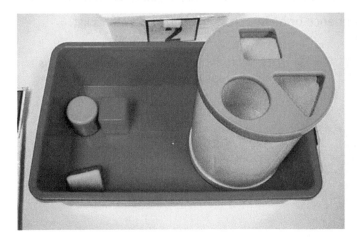

*H9. In this example, the teacher only expects the child to put three shapes into the shape sorter, so there are only three shapes in the box.*

*H10. In this task, there are only as many erasers as will fit in the slots allotted in the container. This provides clear information to the student that she will be finished when all the items are placed in the container. The student puts the basketball erasers in the top row and the footballs in the bottom row.*

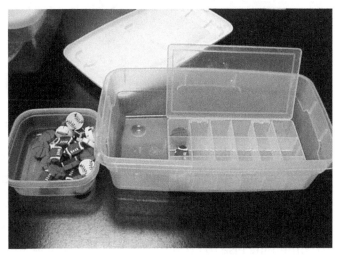

## How Do I Know When I Am Finished?

The student knows he is finished with his work in one of two ways: (a) He knows that he is done when he has moved each of the completed tasks to the "finished" basket or area and there are no tasks left on his work space. (b) If using a visual work schedule, he knows he has finished when there are no more symbols representing tasks left in the sequence or he has crossed everything off his list.

*H11. When the desk is clear and the schedule is empty, the student knows the work is completed.*

## What Do I Do Next?

Individuals with ASD and similar disorders do best when they know what the expectations are. When they have finished their assigned tasks at the structured work area, they need information about where to go or what to do next. When structured work is assigned as one of the areas in a center rotation and the student finishes before it is time to change stations, he should be directed to something else to do in that area. For example, there may be a box of small fidget toys to play with, a book to look at, or a puzzle to complete. These items should be represented by a symbol on the task strip or to the right of the last task basket the child needs to complete. There also may be a symbol directing the child to check his schedule, which will take him to his visual schedule and the next area of the room or activity he needs to participate in. Sometimes the individual may be prompted by a symbol to take a break following the task sequence. In that case, she may be directed to a separate break area or to just sit and relax in the structured work area. Some instructors use a symbol to cue the individual to raise her hand to have an instructor check her work and let her know if she can proceed to her reinforcing activities.

# STRUCTURED WORK SYSTEMS IN SCHOOL SETTINGS:
## CURRICULA, IEPs, AND LESSON PLANNING

Structured work systems are useful for practicing and generalizing previously mastered skills in the areas of fine-motor, cognition-preacademics, language concepts, constructive play, academics (reading, math, and writing), and vocational tasks. In school settings, these skills can be aligned with commonly used classroom curricula. Due to the nature of the available curricula, it is easier to do this for early childhood and primary grades than for intermediate and secondary grades. That is, curriculum tasks for younger students tend to be more hands-on and make use of more manipulative materials, while tasks for older students or adults tend to be more paper- and pencil-based. Students working on an academic curriculum can benefit from the same principles, but the format of their system may be tailored to break down academic tasks assigned in the classroom. As students age, and the system is applied to real-life vocational tasks, it is easier to see the need for these types of systems. Charts depicting skills from published curricula that are appropriate for structured work systems may be found in Appendix B.

For all the reasons previously discussed, structured work systems provide a mechanism to help maintain skills and move toward independence. Some students benefit from having goals and objectives for independence integrated into their individualized education program (IEP). Similarly, some adults benefit from having them integrated into transition plans or habilitation plans.

For students such as Joey (see page 1), a goal might be written for completing one task independently from start to finish. For other individuals, such as Ben (see page 1), the goals and objectives might focus on increasing the amount of work or the length of time they can work independently. Shandra (see page 1), and individuals who are older, may have goals that focus on generalizing their independent skills into the community or workplace.

In addition, all students may have goals in their IEP or habilitation/service plan that focus on specific skills that can be practiced and maintained after mastery in the structured work system. These students would learn the IEP skill with explicit instruction in the classroom and, once the skill is mastered, they would continue to practice it in the structured work system.

Ideas and suggestions for IEP or habilitation plan goals and objectives are provided on page 17. Keep in mind that not everybody who can benefit from structured work systems needs a goal written into their plan. For many, it would be considered part of their curriculum or a beneficial teaching strategy. For students who are extremely dependent upon classmates and teachers, it is critical that special focus be placed on independent functioning. These students would benefit from having a specific goal toward working independently in their IEPs. Working independently is an important skill for all students as the ability to work on their own is key to opening opportunities in the school, home, and community.

### Structured Work Systems and Common Core Curriculum Standards

In light of the increasing need to focus on academic capability and high expectations for all students, including those with disabilities, it is important for teachers working with students with ASD to select instructional strategies that allow their students to increase their skills in reading, the language arts, and mathematics. IDEA requires that students with disabilities have access to accommodations and modifications that ensure access to the common curriculum. Accommodations are changes in the presentation or organization of materials that allow a student to complete work within the state or common core standards. Accommodations do not change the content of the work but allow students to access the curriculum.

For some students who are able to meet the core standards expectations, structured work systems can serve as an evidence-based practice that accommodates their learning. In this situation, the material in the work system would include work that meets the state's curriculum standards or the common core standards. For instance, for students who are able to complete worksheets and other paper and pencil tasks independently, structured work systems provide an organizational structure that promotes independent performance by making clear the steps of an assignment that needs to be completed. Any standard in the common core that can be addressed through paper and pencil can be included in a structured work system. For students who require that the standards be modified or that the state's access standards be employed, a structured work system provides the organization of materials and visual clarity to enable independent performance of the modified work.

## IEP Goals/Objectives Related to Structured Work

Goal 1: When provided with a previously mastered task, the student will take the task out of the basket, complete it, and place it in the "finished" basket independently. Mastery is 90% of the steps being completed independently on 5/5 days.

Goal 2: When provided with one previously mastered task and a one-task visual schedule, the student will match the schedule symbol to the task basket, take the task out of the basket, complete it independently, and place it in the "finished" basket independently. Mastery is 90% of the steps being completed independently on 5/5 days.

Goal 3: When provided with two previously mastered tasks and a two-task visual schedule, the student will complete both tasks in the prescribed order by matching the first schedule symbol to the first task basket, taking the task out of the basket, completing it independently, and placing it in the "finished" basket, and then completing the second task in the same way. Mastery is 90% of the steps being completed independently on 5/5 days.

Goal 4: When provided with three previously mastered tasks and a three-task visual schedule, the student will complete all tasks in the prescribed order by matching the first schedule symbol to the first task basket, taking the task out of the basket, completing it independently, and placing it in the "finished" basket. The individual then completes the second and third tasks in the same way. Mastery is 90% of the steps being completed independently on 5/5 days.

Goal 5: When provided with four previously mastered tasks and a four-task visual schedule, the student will complete all tasks in the prescribed order by matching the first schedule symbol to the first task basket, taking the task out of the basket, completing it independently, and placing it in the "finished" basket. The individual then completes the subsequent tasks in the same way. Mastery is 90% of the steps being completed independently on 5/5 days.

### Other Ideas for Goals

1. Increase time student works at a structured work station.
2. Increase time student works independently.
3. Increase distance of the task's location so student has to leave his seat to get and put away work.
4. Increase number of items in each basket.
5. Increase number of tasks that are completed independently.
6. Set the system up so that it is missing an item or requires that the student ask for additional materials or assistance to encourage communication skills.

### Objectives for Structured Work Goals (These objectives would be used with a selected goal above to identify short-term indicators of progress toward the larger goal.)

1. Increase number of steps that the student must complete independently.
2. Decrease level of prompting – physical, gestural only.
3. Increase time student is able to work at the structured work station.
4. Increase distance of the task's location so student has to move to get and put away work.
5. Proceed to next task by following the "what comes next" visual on task schedule.
6. Keep self occupied by accessing activity or reinforcer by following the "what comes next" visual on task sequence.

The curricula discussed here all include an assessment component. As the instructor plans the schedule and lessons, she integrates the curriculum with each individual's goals. As part of this planning, she determines which skills are best addressed using a structured work system. In this connection, it is important to identify what skills the individual student can perform independently and what skills should be taught next.

Once these assessments are completed for each student, the instructor creates a list of mastered tasks to be included in the structured work area to support maintenance and generalization. The Structured Work Assignment Planning Form (see page 19) may be used to organize the tasks for each individual to complete in this area. It may be useful to number each task so that the staff can quickly and easily pull the correct tasks for each student, especially when several are working at the same table/desk.

As a result of Joey's Level I *Strategies for Teaching Based on Autism Research (STAR)* (Arick, Loos, Falco, & Krug, 2003) assessment and teacher observation, it was found that he was not able to complete any of the basic matching skills under the receptive language concepts domain independently. These included matching object to object, matching picture to picture, and matching object to picture. He also was not able to complete the matching colors and matching shapes skills independently under the pre-academic concepts domain. In addition, he was having difficulty using a visual schedule to transition from activity to activity without prompting. Consequently, it was decided that Joey was not ready to follow a task schedule while doing structured work. The only tasks that he was able to do independently were simple put-in tasks, so it was decided that he was to complete only one simple put-in task while at structured work and that the task would be on the desk for him to complete. In short, he was to complete the one task and place it in a "finished" basket to his right.

To show what a structured work system for another student at a slightly more advanced level would look like, let's introduce Caryn. She has mastered all of the skills in Level I STAR and is beginning to work on Level II STAR skills during small-group instructional time with the teacher. Her current target in receptive language includes sorting by category. In the pre-academic concepts domain, skills targeted consist of tracing her name, letters, and numbers; coloring within lines; and cutting and pasting. A target in the functional routines domain is for Caryn to transition between activities using a schedule. It was decided that Caryn's tasks would include a put-in task, a matching identical pictures task, and coloring within the lines of a simple form task. Further, she would use a task schedule on her left that required her to match colors and have a "finished" basket on her right.

## Structured Work Assignment Planning Form

Date: 5/19/12

| Child's Name | Task One | Task Two | Task Three |
|---|---|---|---|
| Joey | Put clothespins in coffee can (put in) | | |
| Caryn | Matching pictures of common objects | Sorting items by color | Coloring a picture of a frog |
| | | | |
| | | | |
| | | | |
| | | | |
| | | | |
| | | | |
| | | | |

Structured work systems can be applied in a variety of settings (e.g., jobsite, classroom, home) and are useful for a number of purposes, including increasing the independence of a student and allowing instructors or parents to focus on other people or duties in the environment while the student works independently. Regardless of their intended function and setting, structured work systems should always be developed and implemented in a planful way, particularly when teaching the use of the system and building to independence. In a school environment, in particular, this includes the need to focus on goals for independence on the IEP and to link to meaningful curricula in order to continue to enhance the student's skills. However, even in non-school environments (e.g., worksites), planning the work that is contained in the system and ensuring that it is appropriate for the worker is a critical element.

# SETTING UP THE SYSTEM

There are clear rules, including consistent elements, for setting up a structured work system that must be followed to ensure that they answer the four fundamental questions discussed in Chapter 2: What work do I need to do? How much work do I need to do? How do I know when I'm finished? What do I do next? The system must begin with assessment and planning for each student to determine how it will be used and what the student's skills are.

## Planning for Structured Work in the Schedule

Structured work is appropriate for individuals of all ages for use at home, at school, and in the workplace. In a special education classroom, a separate area of the room is often dedicated to structured work. In a general education classroom, the student's desk typically serves as the work area, or a separate area or desk is designated as such. At home, the kitchen table or counter may serve as a structured work area for a child to complete a set of tasks while a parent is cooking dinner. On a job site, a structured work system may be used to organize the tasks that make up the employee's daily jobs.

As a method for teaching individuals with ASD to work independently and to maintain and generalize learned material, structured work should be completed on at least a daily basis. For many, structured work offers a break from adults and staff directly placing demands on them. For that reason, some benefit from having it alternate with more explicit instruction to maintain engagement in learning tasks for longer periods of the day. Other students, such as Joey, benefit from having multiple opportunities to practice the skill within their daily schedule.

The amount of time that is allotted for structured work will vary based on age and skill level. Younger children with fewer independent skills and shorter attention spans may participate in structured work for 5-10 minutes and may engage in a given activity multiple times in a day. High school students, such as Shandra (see page 1), and adults who have a wider variety of independent skills may work independently for 30-45 minutes dependent on the situation.

Structured work can be set up so that everybody in the environment works simultaneously. This requires that a structured work area be set up for each student. Another option is to set up rotations through a structured work time, so that two or three persons work independently at a time among other rotations, including direct instruction, leisure activities, and academic times. This requires fewer structured work stations in the room, only enough to accommodate the greatest number of individuals in a center at one time. The number of stations would depend on the number of students completing a work system simultaneously.

*Throughout the book, many of the tasks and work schedules featured are created from Mayer-Johnson's Boardmaker® software (http://www.mayer-johnson.com). Boardmaker® offers a number of software products that provide collections of pictures/symbols that can be used with individuals with special needs in a variety of ways. Other sets of symbols are also commercially available, or you can use images from the Internet or draw your own.*

## Arranging the Physical Environment (SU)

When designing the work environment, it is important to think about creating an area(s) where individuals can work without being distracted by others or by activities that are taking place at the same time. Often, structured work areas are developed so that the worker has her back to the rest of the room to avoid distractions. Structured work areas can also be segregated from other areas of the room by using furniture to create visual barriers. For example, portable dividers can be moved to reduce or eliminate visual distractions when needed. Individual study carrels can be used for students who need their own work area enclosed on all sides. For instance, Joey needs an area away from distractions. Ben can complete his work system at his desk in the general education classroom, while Shandra completes a work system on the job site or in an area of the classroom designated for that task.

One decision that must be made is whether a separate work area is needed or whether two can share a table that is divided into separate areas. The available furniture may be a determining factor in that decision. Furthermore, it is likely that each person in the room has different tasks to do during this time. Sometimes the work areas can be set up to meet the needs of several persons performing on similar levels. For example, three structured work areas may be set up: one for the those with more advanced skills, one for a middle group, and one for the those who are more challenged.

Another decision that must be made related to the physical environment is where the worker will be when the completed work system is reset. Never reset the system (i.e., undo the work) while the worker watches, as this may be interpreted to mean that the finished product was not meaningful. It is also important to think about where the worker will complete her "what's next?" task. Should it be at the same location? If so, the staff will reset after the worker leaves. Or should it be at a different table or area of the room (e.g., going to the computer as a reinforcer for completion) so that the staff can reset the systems for the next set of workers in the absence of the individual who just left?

*SU1. In this situation, there are two tables side by side with work systems. The first three baskets are tasks to be completed; the fourth basket contains reinforcing toys for the preschooler completing the system. The child sits facing the wall to limit distractions and places finished work in the bin on the floor.*

*SU2. This teacher used science lab tables as work tables for her middle school students as these were available to her. This setup consists of three tables set up in a U-shape, with one against the wall for a student who is distracted by other activities in the classroom.*

SU3. In this set of systems, the students face toward the wall, and each is working with a system that contains three baskets. Students who are less distractible can be seated farthest from the wall, while those who are more distractible can be directly facing the wall. All students place finished work on a shelf on the right, which is out of the picture.

SU4. This instructor only had access to a round table. To provide enough stations for the class, she divided the table using colored tape and set each side up for a different system. The student using this system will complete two baskets and place them in the "finished" basket to the right on the floor. At another time of day, two students could work at the same table facing each other with two systems.

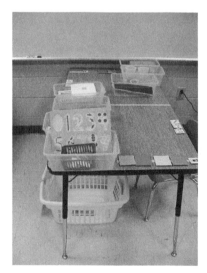

SU5. This instructor had a limited number of tables, so the class used a longer table to house two systems. The students sit on opposite sides of the table to accommodate table size and student distractibility.

SU6. This instructor put two desks together to create a structured work area. The student's name is in the top-left corner of the desk indicating it is his work station along with the visual he uses to check in with his picture from his schedule. Before beginning each task, the student matches the numbers to the baskets so he knows what to complete. He then places the completed task in the laundry basket on the floor to his right.

SU7. A large table can be divided in two using masking tape; one student can sit on each end.

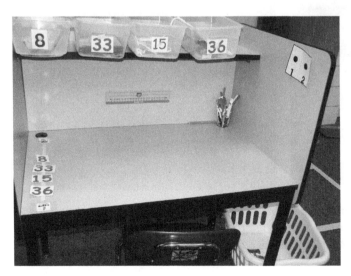

SU8. This instructor used library carrels to set up structured work systems. This works well for students who are easily distracted by other activities in the classroom.

## Task Storage

Another consideration is whether the worker needs his work on a work table or whether tasks can be stored in a separate shelving unit or area of the room. For example, if he needs to have his work on his desk to prevent him from wandering away from the area and not complete his task, the table surface must be deep enough to both hold the task baskets and provide a work-space on which the individual completes the task.

Students who have more independent skills can travel to a separate area of the room where tasks are organized and stored. The tasks may be organized by individual or type of task, and tasks not currently being used may be placed in storage bags, in plastic bins on shelves, or in closets out of the way.

*SU9. This cubby for preschoolers houses the tasks for their work systems with ready-made pictures to add to the schedules as they are pulled for the individual systems.*

*SU10. On the left is a work supply shelf in a high school program. The students follow a schedule to get the baskets from the shelf, take them to their work station at the tables (unseen forefront of photo), complete them, put them on a separate shelf (photo on the right), and return to the work supply shelf for their next task.*

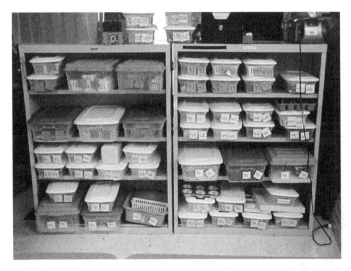

*SU11. This is a work supply shelf in a high school classroom. The students follow a schedule to get the baskets from the shelf, take them to their desks, complete them, put them in a laundry basket to the right of their desks, and return for their next task. Each basket shows two numbers: one that stays on the basket for the student to match and one that the instructor uses to create the student's schedule or task list when setting up the assignments.*

*SU12. This is a storage system for a middle school classroom. The tasks are all numbered and correspond to the students' written schedules. The shelf is located behind the students' work system carrels, so they must go to the shelf to get the material on their lists. The curtains below the baskets cover the teacher's work materials that are stored on the shelves.*

*SU13. This is another example of a shelf from which the students get their assigned tasks. Each student has a list of tasks to complete, and all the containers are numbered. As pictured here, a variety of containers may be appropriate for different types of tasks, including binders and recipe/file card boxes.*

If a separate area of the room is used for structured work, it is important to label it clearly. This can include posting a picture of the area that matches the visual schedules that the students are using, as pictured below. A check-in board or envelope should be available in the area for students who take their schedule piece to each activity. Each student would check his or her schedule and may take a visual of the structured work area (e.g., photo or line drawing) and match it to a similar or identical picture in the area to check in.

*SU14. This check-in envelope has a matching picture and a matching word cue for the workers to use. The majority of the participants were using a picture schedule, whereas one individual employed a written schedule that he moved when he transitioned. The envelope makes it easy to use the check-in device for multiple areas during the day without having to clear off a board. It also makes it easy to gather the visuals at the end of the day to reset the schedules.*

## The Work Schedule

The work schedule tells what work needs to be done and in what order. The schedule is always organized in a top-to-bottom or left-to-right sequence. The youngest students, like Joey, may not use a separate schedule or list of tasks. Their work is usually just presented on the work surface and may start as simply as one task basket. As students learn to understand the meaning of a visual task list, a sequence of symbols may be used to tell them what work to do. These symbols may first be introduced as three-dimensional objects, or as other tangible symbols for workers who do not yet understand two-dimensional symbols. A variety of two-dimensional symbols can be used to represent the work sequence: pictures of common objects, colors, shapes, numbers, and letters. Each symbol on the schedule should be duplicated and attached to the container of the corresponding task (see SU11).

For students such as Ben, who are able to read, the schedule may be a written list of the actual tasks (see SU17). Symbols are selected based on age and developmental level and can be rotated to match thematic units in the classroom; for example, different-colored butterflies may be used as symbols for a young child when the class is reading *The Very Hungry Caterpillar* or using that as a theme for instruction. Remember that the schedule should include an indication of what the student is to do when he has finished his work. For somebody who is visually impaired, a tactile symbol should be put on the inside of the box so they can feel the symbol as they grab the side of the task box.

*SU15. In this schedule, the student matches letter cards to identical cards on the bins and gets M&Ms for completing his work.*

*SU16. In this schedule, an edible is found in the small container at the end of the schedule for a child who better understands the reinforcer if represented by an object. This system might be good for Joey and could be used in an early childhood class with "Teddy Bears' Picnic" (children's song) theme.*

*SU17. This middle school student has a written schedule on a card listing numbered baskets to complete. He can manage seven baskets in one session. On this student's daily schedule, following the index card with the work schedule would be a card that indicated his next activity. This system might be good for Shandra.*

SU18. In this schedule, the student knows to check for the next task when his work is completed. Notice that the tasks are placed left to right while the schedule is positioned top to bottom. The tasks are located on the left to help him begin to transition to getting his tasks from a storage area away from his desk.

SU19. In this example, a computer visual at the bottom of the schedule on the left side of the table indicates that the student gets to spend time on the computer as a reinforcer for completing her work. The computer is often a preferred reinforcer for individuals with ASD; it may be a good idea to situate the computer area near the structured work area.

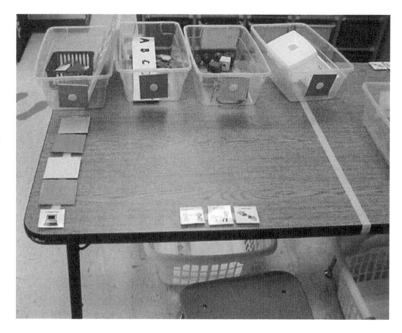

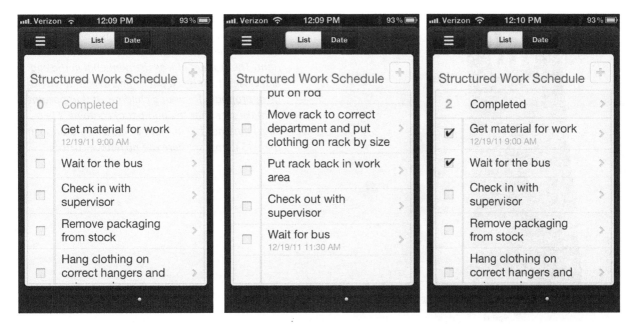

*SU20. This set of pictures show a schedule using the Reminders app on an iPhone for somebody who is working in a store. The first two pictures show the list of tasks she must complete – the first includes a reminder that will make a noise and pop up when it is time to start work and another that will remind her when it is time to get on the bus at the end of her shift. The third picture shows how the schedule would look as she checks off items when they are completed. (Reminders is an Apple app that is standard on all iPhones, iPod Touches, and iPads using IOS 5.0 or later.)*

## Task Organization (TO)

As mentioned, the tasks that are included in structured work systems should be previously mastered tasks. This means that the worker has already been taught the task through explicit instruction and has reached an independent mastery level. Individuals with ASD often do not maintain skills or fail to apply them to new materials or environments. Structured work provides an opportunity to practice skills on a regular basis and use similar, but not identical, materials to ensure generalization across environments and materials.

Tasks must be organized and presented in a way that is visually clear. The worker should be able to take the task basket and, just by looking at the materials placed within, be able to complete the task without assistance. Many tasks are best organized using a variety of small plastic containers or notebooks. For instance, each material in an assembly job would have its own container.

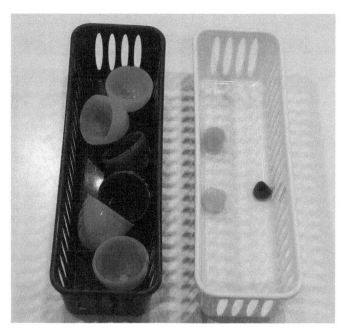

*TO1. In this example, a young child picks up the matching halves of the plastic eggs from the left and finds the matching colored pom pom on the right. The student places the pom pom in the egg and closes it. This is a packaging task that would be appropriate for young children. It is important to make sure that the number of containers (e.g., 3 eggs) matches the number of materials that go in them (3 items) so there are no leftover pieces.*

*TO2. In this example, the employee is packaging toiletries. Resealable plastic zipper bags sit to the left of the bin (out of the picture). The employee works clockwise to put one tube of toothpaste, one shampoo bottle, one comb, and one bar of soap in each bag before placing the completed toiletry kit in the basket to the right (out of the picture.)*

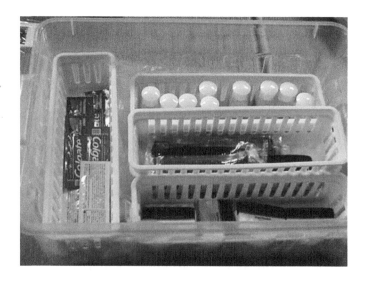

## The "Finished" Area (F)

Workers need to have a "finished" area to place their tasks as they complete each one. Often, a laundry basket or large plastic container is placed to the right of the worker, as he is taught to always work from left to right and top to bottom (as seen in F1). This structure would be appropriate for Joey, for example. For individuals who are more independent and under better behavioral control, such as Shandra, the tasks can be moved to a separate "finished" area in the room and the teacher can check the accuracy of the work at a later time (as seen in F2 and F3). For students in a general education classroom, such as Ben, the "finished" area could be an inbox on the teacher's desk or the right side of a pocket folder (as seen in F4).

*F1. Typically, the basket has a "finished" sign on it. This can consist of the word "finished" and/ or a picture from Mayer-Johnson's Boardmaker® indicating "finished." Some teachers use the "all done" visual and words instead. Laundry baskets make good "finished" baskets because they are large enough to contain the work and the bins that often contain it.*

*F2. This is a "finished" area for a student who gets her work from a shelf and travels to put it in a centralized finished area. All the students put their finished work on this table.*

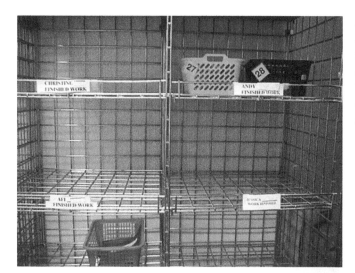

F3. This is a "finished" shelf system for high school students referred to earlier (SU10). The students get their work from a different work shelf, take it to their seat, complete it, and then return it to this shelf. Sections of the shelf are marked with students' names to indicate where their work is to be placed for easy checking by the teacher.

F4. This system was designed for a student in a general education setting. The work to be completed is on the left under "to do" and the "finished" work is placed in the right-hand pocket.

# SELECTING WORK TASKS

As mentioned throughout, tasks selected for structured work systems must be tasks that the individual has mastered and can complete without assistance. Therefore, tasks and materials vary by grade and age/developmental level of the workers. Some tasks are more academically oriented while others are functionally oriented. Work systems are appropriate for all ages of individuals. Preschoolers may work on tasks that are developmentally appropriate while adults would work on tasks that are related to a job site. Tasks are developed to meet individual goals, and work materials might be age appropriate and reflect the overall goals of the individual program.

For instance, because Shandra is transitioning to a vocational setting, her work systems will consist of tasks from potential job sites. For jobs in clerical settings, Shandra may work on filing tasks. For working at a restaurant, her tasks might involve filling salt and pepper shakers. For Ben, his work would be more academic and usually more paper- and pencil-oriented, as a student who is in the general education classroom. It would also reflect the assignments he has worked on in the past. The tasks may be the same as or different from what the other students are doing in the general education classroom.

## Common Materials for Creating Structured Work Tasks

Work tasks may be created from a variety of materials that are readily available commercially or may be assembled from recycled materials. The following is a partial list.

### All Levels

Plastic containers of all shapes and sizes to hold components of tasks (e.g., Tupperware®, margarine containers, GladWare®)
File folders
Library pockets
Velcro®
Laminator and laminate to protect file folders and task pieces
Dry erase markers and erasers
Plastic or cardboard shoeboxes
Laundry baskets
Ice cube trays
Styrofoam trays for organizing materials or cut-out templates
Egg cartons
Potato chip cans
Plastic zipper bags
Popsicle® sticks
Worksheets

### Preschool/Primary

Spring-loaded clothespins
Poker chips
Variety of math manipulatives for sorting (e.g., counting bears)
Lotto games for matching
Pegs and pegboards
Jigsaw puzzles
Beads and strings
Lacing cards
Dressing boards
Sequencing cards
Legos® for assembly
Pop beads for assembly
Plastic eggs
Picture cards
Worksheets

### Intermediate/Secondary/Adult

Pieces of wood
Hammer
Nails (different sizes)
Phillips head screwdriver,
Regular screwdriver
Phillips head wood screws
Regular head wood screws
Pieces of wood, saw
Flashlights and batteries
Variety of pens for sorting and/or assembly
Pencils and cap erasers
Nuts and bolts to assemble or disassemble
Variety of buttons to sort by color, shape, size
3 x 5 inch file boxes, file cards, and dividers (numbers, letters, blank)
4 x 6 inch file boxes, file cards, and dividers (numbers, letters, blank)
Paper clips, large and small
Staplers
Brads
Film canisters or empty pill bottles
Business size envelopes (number 10)
Address labels
Price tags
Coin wrappers
Greeting cards and envelopes
Plastic hair curlers of various sizes for sorting and assembly
Toothbrushes and cases for assembly
Salt and pepper shakers, salt, pepper, and funnel
Creamer, sugar, and sweetener packets, stirrers, and bags
Washcloths for folding
Variety of pairs of socks for matching
Rice for measuring
Measuring cups
Coins
Rulers

Tasks for work systems can be developed to meet different skill levels, such as categorizing and clerical tasks.  Tasks can be designed to meet both academic and functional types of skills. As emphasized throughout, it is important to only select tasks that have already been mastered so they can be completed independently. In addition ...

- Tasks should have a clear beginning and end so that the worker knows when the task is complete.
- Tasks should be organized within the containers in which they are stored so that task expectations are clearly understood.
- Finally, tasks should be designed so that they remain assembled when placed in the "finished" container or area. Containers that close or use Velcro® to attach pieces are recommended for this purpose. This allows the instructor to check an individual's work and also allows the worker to move on after completing a task because it does not disassemble.

The remainder of this chapter presents tasks from different categories. Within each category, tasks are organized by the age/developmental level for which they are appropriate (e.g., preschool/primary, intermediate/secondary/adults). Because many tasks are appropriate for multiple areas, a chart cross-listing tasks with areas and age is available at the end of each section.  Beside each heading is a code that references corresponding pictures.

## Put-In Tasks (PI)

For children, such as Joey, who are just beginning to work independently, tasks involving putting objects into containers are generally good choices. They can vary from placing plastic chips in a coffee can to putting plastic cookies into a cookie jar; slotting pegs into pegboards to taking clothespins off the rim of a coffee can and putting them inside; or completing puzzles in which the student must discriminate the items that are put into the designated holes.

## Preschool/Primary

PI1. Simple form boards and puzzles are good put-in tasks for young children. If a child has difficulty discriminating the shapes, leave three of the pieces in the puzzle and have her put in the missing piece. Then slowly build the number of pieces she can put in independently. This task is good for children with fine-motor difficulty as the pieces are three-dimensional.

PI2. Putting clothespins in a coffee can is a basic put-in task that is easy to develop and set up. In this example, students do not have to unclip the clothespins so it is suitable for somebody who has limited fine-motor strength. Students take the clothespin off and place it in the can. The number of clothespins can be tailored to the individual's level of independence so that somebody with less ability to work independently would have fewer clothespins to put in the can.

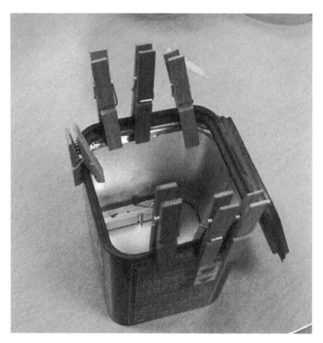

PI3. This task is a replication of the clothespin task above using the more traditional clothespins that require pinching to complete the task. The students unclip the clothespins and put them in the can.

PI4. Putting blocks in a hole is another simple put-in task. The Velcro® holding the blocks on top of the bin organizes the task, with a clear space to put the block into the box. When the student is finished, the blocks stay in the box – giving a clear cue that when the blocks are gone from the top of the box, the task is finished.

PI5. Tasks can be developed for seasonal, thematic, or special interests. This task requires putting one pumpkin eraser in each plastic pumpkin. It was designed for a student who needed to practice picking up small items and 1:1 correspondence and was developed for Halloween.

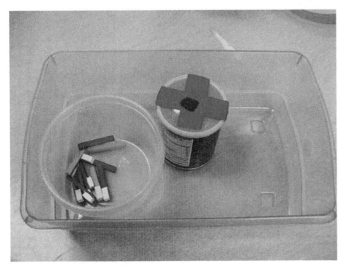

PI6. This task involves putting toothbrush-shaped erasers through a hole in a potato chip can. The container holds the erasers so they are centrally located and the student doesn't miss any of them when placing them in the can. When the bowl is empty, the task is completed.

*PI7. Popsicle® sticks in potato chip cans are another example of a put-in task. In this example, the student has to push the stick through the slot rather than just dropping it in.*

Shoebox Tasks® from Centering on Children are available from www.shoeboxtasks.com. They are simple tasks that are made to be self-contained (i.e., the entire task fits within its own bin). The tasks are constructed in white shoebox-like containers and give clear cues about the work that is expected for a given task. The tasks can be reversed (e.g., so that materials can be put into a container or taken out of a container). These types of tasks have the advantage that all the materials are arranged in a stable way so that the students do not have to be concerned with how to rearrange the materials by taking them out of the box. Below are several examples of Shoebox Tasks®.

*PI8. This is a simple task involving putting balls in the hole. When the bin of balls is empty, the task is complete. This type of task provides very clear cues. This is a Shoebox Task® early in the developmental series.*

PI9. This task involves taking beads off a stick and putting them in the container. The stick should contain only the number of beads that are expected to be removed and put in the container. The task can be reversed so that the student takes the blocks out of the container and places them on the stick.

PI10. This is a simple task that involves taking the pegs out of a pegboard and putting them in a bowl. Like many of these types of tasks, it can be reversed by taking the pegs out of the container and putting them on the pegboard.

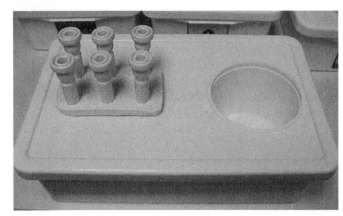

PI11. This task requires simply taking the pegs out of the bowl and putting them through the holes. This task begins work on 1:1 correspondence of one peg to each hole. This task can also be reversed.

*PI12. For fine-motor skills in addition to put-in skills, this task requires picking up toy spiders with tweezers and putting them in the container on the right through a small hole in the lid. This requires precise fine-motor skills and could be used with older students or adults.*

*PI13. Ice cube trays and egg cartons make good structures for beginning 1:1 correspondence. In this task, the student puts one kitten in each hole of the tray. This helps him learn to isolate his putting-in actions and begin to sort materials. One of the kittens has been placed in the first slot of the ice tray.*

*PI14. Putting whiffle balls or tennis balls in muffin tins makes a good put-in task. Any object may be used in place of the balls based on the chronological/developmental age or special interest of the worker.*

PI15. Putting chips through a slot is another simple structured work task that can be created with everyday, inexpensive materials. This task was created with paper cups, tops with a slit, and counters bought at an office supply store. The chips may be taken out of the cup on the left and placed through the slot in the cup on the right.

PI16. For young children, holiday items are a cheap and easy way to stock materials for structured work systems. These bunny tongs and the egg tray make a good put-in task for a young child with the addition of puffs. The child picks up the pom poms with the tongs and places them in the egg-shaped space on the right.

## Intermediate/Secondary/Adult

PI17. This is a variation of a put-in task for older individuals for whom swallowing small objects is not a concern. The individual takes the marbles and puts them in the detergent bottle. The use of more functional materials, such as the laundry detergent bottle, also fits with the focus of training for older individuals.

*PI18. Filling peat pots or small pots with potting soil is an adaptation of the put-in task for older individuals in need of more functional skills. Workers fill the pots and place them upright in a container that is placed in the finished area or box.*

*PI19. Using templates for put-in tasks is a good way to begin to teach how to discriminate between sorting bins in later tasks. This task involves putting bottles into a bin for recycling; it is appropriate for secondary-level students and adult workers. The cutout (template) at the top gives visual information about what types of material go into the bin, which can be helpful to expand to a sorting task at a later time.*

*PI20. Putting golf tees in a cribbage board is a good fine-motor put-in task for somebody whose skills are rudimentary.*

*PI21. Putting pencils in a can is a good put-in task*

*emphasizing the fine-motor skills required to accurately place an object in a hole.*

**Cross-Listing of Tasks by Age/Developmental Level for Put-In Tasks**

| Category | Preschool/Primary | Intermediate/Secondary/Adult |
|---|---|---|
| **Put-In** | H9, PI1, PI2, PI3, PI4, PI5, PI6, PI7, PI8, PI9, PI10, PI11, PI12, PI13, PI14, PI15, PI16, PI20, PI21, SC14, P2 | PI12, PI6, PI7, PI14, PI15, PI17, PI18, PI19, PI20, PI21, P2 |

## Matching (M)

Matching tasks are excellent for beginning learners who are able to match common objects or pictures. File folder tasks (that is, instructional activities that are self-contained within a file folder) and lotto or bingo games work well for these types of tasks and allow for significant variety. Things can be matched on a variety of dimensions – color, size, number, letter, pattern, word, or category – and can be matched simultaneously (color and shape) dependent on skill level. Similarly, items can be matched across dimensions, such as matching pictures to written words. The visual clarity of matching tasks, the ability to expand to different levels of skill, and the ability to fasten the matching pieces together easily in most cases make these tasks ideal for structured work systems.

## Preschool/Primary

M1. This task involves matching pictures of identical animals and fastening the pictures together with Velcro®. This task would be appropriate for a preschool student working on a unit about farm animals.

M2. Tasks can be chosen to match holiday or theme-related activities. This file folder game requires matching presents by their shape and pattern rather than by their color. With another set of manipulatives, this activity could be set up to match identical colors or shapes. (Velcro® keeps the pieces attached when the student puts the folder in the "finished" basket.)

M3. Lotto games, such as the one here from Frank Shaffer Publications available at most school supply stores, make excellent material for matching tasks in work systems. In this case, pictures are matched to those on the lotto card. The pictures are attached to the card with Velcro® to prevent them from falling off when the task is placed in the "finished" area.

M4. This task requires both matching and fine-motor ability. Students must match by color and shape. This task was purchased from Lakeshore Learning (http://www.lakeshorelearning.com).

M5. This task requires matching vehicles for a transportation unit that would be appropriate for preschool/primary children.

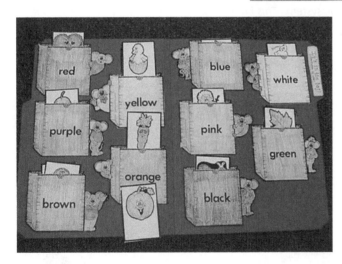

M6. This commercially available Carson-Dellosa (www.carsondellosa.com/) file folder activity requires matching the color of pictured objects to the labeled pictures of the bags of the corresponding colors. The manipulative pieces tuck in a pocket to stay together when the folder is closed.

M7. Here is a Carson-Dellosa file folder (www.carsondellosa.com/ ) for matching shapes. Other folders in the series include matching circles, squares, and triangles. Items are either matched by size of the shapes or by colors. In this example, the matching task is two-dimensional —both the type of shape and the color or size of the shape have to be matched. The pieces should be affixed to the file folder with Velcro® and can be stored in a clear plastic bag taped to the back of the folder.

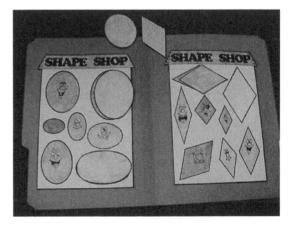

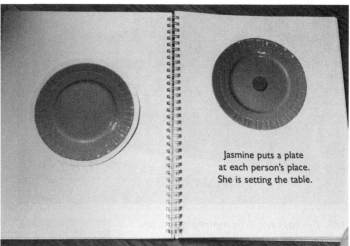

Jasmine puts a plate
at each person's place.
She is setting the table.

M8. This book is from a series of books that include matching photographs of functional objects as part of a story. Students can read the story and match the pictures as part of their work system after it has been read to the group or during a reading activity. The pictures are stored either in the book when matched or in an envelope or plastic bag attached to the back of the book. If the pictures are stored on the pictures in the book, they should be removed and placed in the bin for the student to match them in the system. This book comes from a set of 10 books available from LinguiSystems (http://www.linguisystems.com). Similar books have also been developed for middle school-aged children and adults with ASD and related disabilities.

M9. This is a winter file folder activity in which the students match pieces to the seasonal pictures. The pieces of the game can be stored in a bag attached to the back of the folder and placed in a bin separate from the file folder for the student to Velcro® onto matching pictures in the folder.

M10. This Carson-Dellosa folder (www.carsondellosa.com/) called "Don't Lose Your Head" requires matching the colored head to the body. This is a simple matching task when the bodies are the same color as the heads. To become more complex, the task may be changed so that the body is white (with the color word written on it) and the head is colored. The students retrieve the item from a bag on the back of the folder and then match the color to the word. The pieces are affixed with Velcro® to the file folder so that the task stays in tact when it is placed in the "finished" basket.

M11. This Carson-Dellosa file folder (www.carsondellosa.com/) involves matching colors. On the left side of the page is a set of colors with corresponding color words. On the right side is a set of colored dots or numerals that can be matched to number words. If the task just requires matching colors, the folder is to be colored so that the corresponding pieces are the same color as the circles. If the task is to match numerals to number words, care should be taken not to give an extra cue by having the pieces and file folder spots be the same color. Pieces may be stored on the back of the folder in a bag that seals and put in the bin for the student to access when the system is set up.

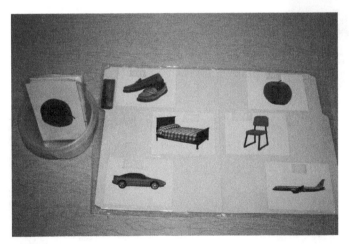

M12. This task requires matching pictures similar to those used in direct instruction. This activity is made with Language Builder: Picture Noun Cards from Stages Learning Materials (www.stageslearning.com). As illustrated, the pictures to be matched are stored in a container (on the left); they are matched to the corresponding picture using the Velcro® on the back of the card and on the folder.

*M13. This Lotto card, from a bingo game by Trend Enterprises (http://trendenterprises.com), requires matching. This type of lotto game is readily available commercially from educational supply stores.*

*M14. This task, made with Mayer-Johnson's Boardmaker® software, requires matching pictures of common objects stored in the bin in the left of the picture.*

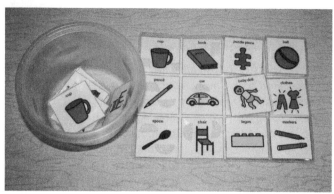

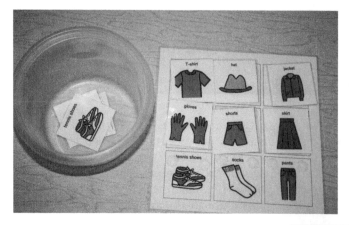

*M15. This matching task (made with Mayer-Johnson's Boardmaker® software) would be good for a thematic unit on clothing or working on dressing skills.*

*M16. This file folder (also made with Mayer-Johnson's Boardmaker® software) requires matching items that will be used in the visual schedule, thus preteaching the matching required in using schedules. The pictures to be matched are placed in a bin off to the left of the folder; they are fastened by Velcro® to the folder so that they stay in place when the task is placed in the "finished" basket.*

*M17. This task requires matching utensils to a place setting to learn skills related to setting the table. The basket keeps the items contained within the task.*

*M18. In this file folder task, crayon pictures are matched to color. Velcro® keeps the pictures in place when the folder is placed in the "finished" basket. The crayon pictures can be stored in a bag on the back of the file folder.*

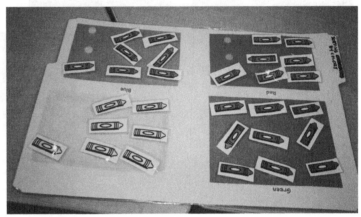

## Intermediate/Secondary/Adult

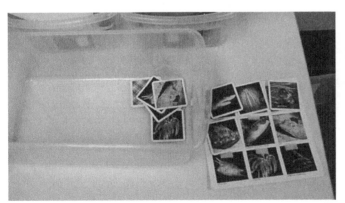

*M19. This task involves matching pictures of sea creatures to identical pictures on a card. This task may be used with individuals who can match more complex patterns. Velcro® keeps the pictures secure when the task is finished.*

M20. In this activity, clothes are matched to the weather depicted in the picture. Pieces are stored on a bag on the back of the task.

M21. This task involves matching stamps of magazines cut from coupons to corresponding pictures of magazines.

M22. This task requires matching fabric swatches of different colors, patterns, and textures to corresponding identical swatches. Workers place each pair of swatches in a plastic bag and put the bag in the "finished" container.

*M23. This task requires matching pairs of socks and rolling them. When rolled, the socks are placed in the "finished" bin.*

*M24. (Above) By using decks of small and large playing cards, this task consists of materials suitable for older individuals who are working on basic matching activities. The large cards are stored in a shoebox bin, and the smaller cards are stored in a smaller container so the worker can easily access the pictures to match them.*

*M25. (Left) This is a visual template used for rolling out dough at a pretzel store. The employee rolls out the dough to match the template.*

### Cross-Listing of Tasks by Age/Developmental Level of Matching Tasks

| Category | Preschool/Primary | Intermediate/Secondary/Adult |
|----------|-------------------|------------------------------|
| **Matching** | M1, M2, M3, M4, M5, M6, M7, M8, M9, M10, M11, M12, M13, M14, M15, M16, M17, M18, SC2, R1, R2, R3, R6, R7, MA1, MA2, MA5, MA6, AD1, AD2, AD3, AD4, AD5, P1, P3, P5 | M8, M12, M16, M19, M20, M21, M22, M23, M24, M25, SC25, SC27, R10, R11, R12, R13, MA8, MA17, MA18, P3, P7 |

## Sorting/Categorizing (SC)

Individuals with autism or related disabilities often need to work on basic skills such as sorting items into categories by color, form, or function. Young children may be sorting toys or preschool manipulatives by color. Adults might be working on sorting mail in an office or sorting ketchup and mustard packets in a restaurant.

The following are examples of sorting tasks by different ages/developmental levels. As with all tasks, it is important to ensure that the materials are appropriate for the age of the individual using the system while also meeting his or her developmental needs.

### *Preschool/Primary*

*SC1. This is a simple color-sorting task requiring the child to put the bears in the cups of the corresponding color.*

*SC2. This task requires sorting Popsicle® sticks by color. The Popsicle® sticks are kept in a resealable plastic bag to prevent them from scattering. The entire task can be completed within the larger container working left to right. When the sorting container is closed, the sticks will stay organized when placed in the "finished" basket.*

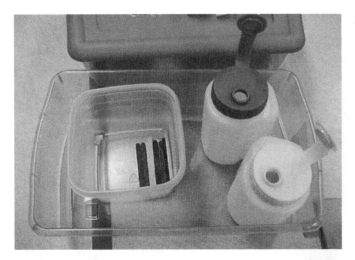

SC3. This is a variation of a simpler sorting task using Popsicle® sticks. This task may also be adapted with one container for a put-in task.

SC4. This task requires sorting erasers of different sports balls, placing each in a separate space. The container on the left holds only those items that fit in the sorter. The sorting container can be closed, ensuring that it will stay organized when placed in the "finished" area. This task would work well for elementary-level students who need more age-appropriate materials than colored bears, for example.

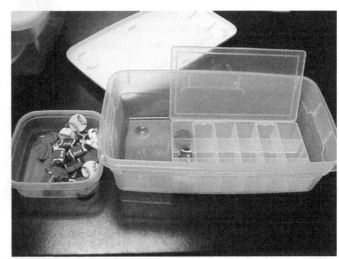

SC5. This task involves sorting blocks by color into matching containers. The containers are made of potato chip cans. This task is made more difficult by requiring that the blocks also be sorted by shape with matching cutouts of shapes in the lids of the corresponding containers.

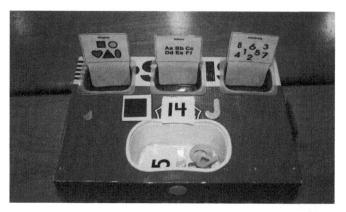

SC6. This task requires sorting shapes, letters, and numbers given a visual cue. The front container in the box stores the mixed materials before they are sorted into the small containers. It is a baby wipes box. The items are sorted into three small baby food containers (these might be replaced by pudding containers). The task is self-contained within a shoebox with holes cut out to keep the materials together.

SC7. This task requires preschool children to sort pictures of classmates by gender. The task is made with a shoebox and baby food or pudding cups as containers. This keeps the task together as one item and requires little organization other than sorting.

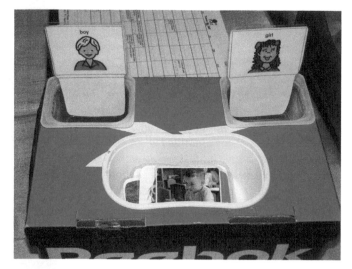

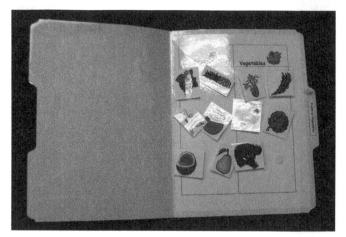

SC8. This task uses pictures obtained through Google Images (http://www.google.com) for sorting fruits from vegetables. Pictures are stored in a bag on the back of the folder.

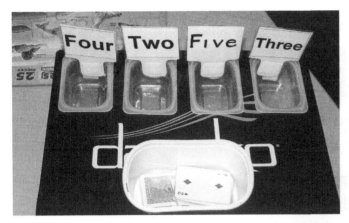

SC9. This task is set up similarly to SC6 and SC7 using baby food containers and a baby wipes case housed within a shoebox. It requires sorting playing cards by matching the numbers on the card to the words.

SC10. Using similar materials, this task requires sorting photographs that show different emotions. The picture symbols (from Mayer-Johnson's Boardmaker® software) serve as a cue for the category.

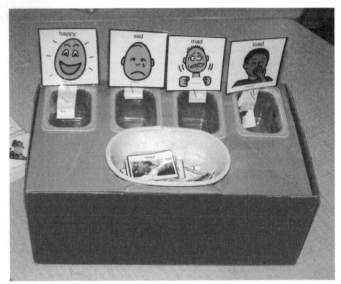

SC11. This task is made up of a shoebox, baby food containers, and a margarine container. It requires sorting pictures of objects into the categories of clothing, food, animals, and toys. (These pictures are also made with Mayer-Johnson's Boardmaker® software.)

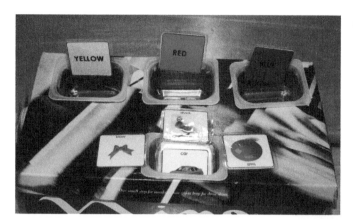

SC12. This task, also self-contained in a shoebox, requires sorting items by color into the appropriate container.

SC13. This is a Carson-Dellosa (www.carsondellosa. com/) file folder activity in which students sort shapes on the crayons by the shapes on the crayon boxes. In this picture, the shapes on the crayon boxes are different colors (e.g., triangles are colored different colors). This makes the task more difficult because students cannot use the colors of the shapes as a cue. To make the task easier, identical shapes could be colored the same color (e.g., all squares are blue) and could match the color of the shapes on the box they are sorted into.

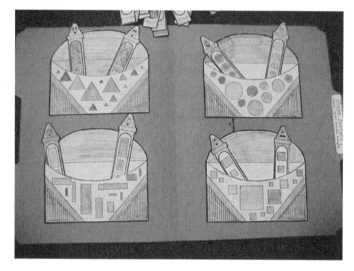

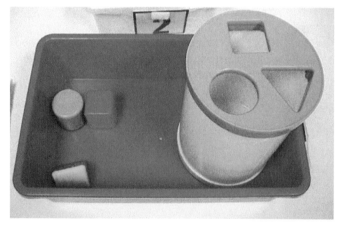

SC14. Shape sorters make great sorting tasks for young children. Limit the number of shapes based on the child's ability and persistence with tasks. This type of task can also be modified to a simple put-in task by covering two of the slots and providing only one shape.

SC15. This task requires sorting clothespins by colors into the bins with matching colored paper in the bottom.

## Intermediate/Secondary/Adult

SC16. This task requires sorting paperclips by color in a muffin tin. Other commonly used items may be used in the same container to sort by type of item, color, or size. An egg carton may be used instead of a muffin tin.

SC17. In this task geared for adults, the labeled laundry baskets are used to sort the light-colored laundry items from the dark-colored items. The laundry to be sorted is located in the laundry basket labeled "Sorting" on the right. Traditionally, the basket of clothes to be sorted would be on the left.

SC18. This task involves sorting clothes and putting them away in a bureau. The drawers are clearly labeled so that the individual knows where to place the various types of clothing.

SC19. This task, appropriate for adults, requires sorting work and non-work types of clothes into different hampers. The work clothes are the uniforms the adults wear to work. Similar tasks may constructed for light and dark laundry.

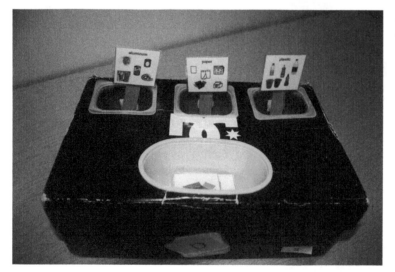

SC20. This self-contained task requires sorting pictures by the type of recycling that would be used for the item depicted (aluminum, paper, and plastic). The task is self-contained in a shoebox with the items to be sorted stored in a baby wipes container. The items are sorted into the three baby food or pudding containers.

SC21. Sorting silverware is a common task used with secondary students and adults to practice sorting and to practice common functional living skills. Silverware may be metal or plastic. A model (as in the picture) or no model may be used, depending on individual skill levels.

SC22. A high school science teacher used coupons and ads and asked students to sort food from nonfood items into the large envelopes. The ads were stored in a third envelope out of the picture.

SC23. (Below) In other science-related tasks, students had to separate pictures of living from nonliving things (left) and liquids from solids (right). The pictures were stored in a bin with the cards. (Several of the nonliving and liquid items shown have already been categorized.)

SC24. This task is a variation on the ones above, requiring sorting pictures of plants and animals and attaching them to the appropriate sheet.

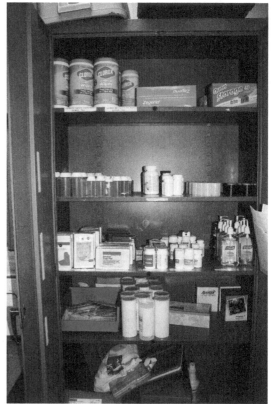

SC25. In this task, employees are stocking a supply closet by putting items into specific spots in the closet that correspond to their items. For instance, all the hand sanitizer bottles are placed on the middle shelf on the right.

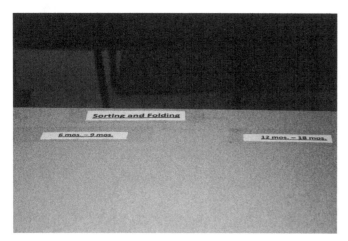

SC26. In this program for 18- to 22-year-olds, participants sort clothes by age range in the areas of the table labeled. This prepares them for tasks at a clothing store where clothes must be placed in the appropriate areas of the racks or shelves. The labels on the table refer to the activity (Sorting and Folding at the top of the table) and spaces for sorting the clothes by age range 8 months to 9 months on the left and 12 months to 18 months on the right.

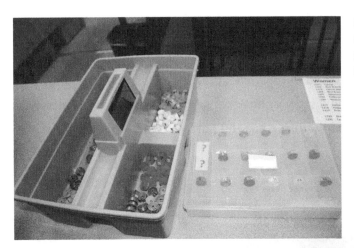

*SC27. This task requires sorting markers for hangers that indicate the size of the clothes. This task prepares an individual to sort hangers with the size indicators on them in a store.*

*SC28. This picture is of the inventory of a school store. Students are told to sort the sodas by type and take inventory based on the numbers on the shelves. They also sell the sodas and restock when the shelves get low.*

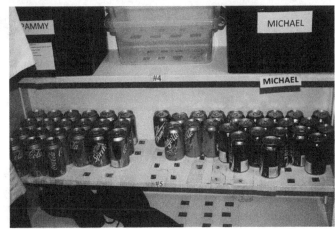

*SC29. This task requires sorting pictures of food items (in the container with the label "9") by food group (onto the pages with the corresponding category picture). The number "9" on the container corresponds to the schedule of the participant, who has matched his "9" to the "9" on the container before completing the task.*

### Cross-Listing of Tasks by Age/Developmental Level for Sorting and Categorizing Tasks

| Category | Preschool/Primary | Intermediate/Secondary/Adult |
|---|---|---|
| Sorting/Categorizing | M18, SC1, SC2, SC3, SC4, SC5, SC6, SC7, SC8, SC9, SC10, SC11, SC12, SC13, SC14, SC15, SC20, SC21, SC24, SC29, P4 | SC4, SC6, SC8, SC9, SC11, SC16, SC17, SC18, SC19, SC20, SC21, SC22, SC23, SC24, SC25, SC26, SC27, SC28, SC29, C3, C4, C5, C7 |

## Sequencing and Patterning (SP)

Sequencing requires arranging materials by time and/or order. At the simplest level, material is put in order of what comes first, second, and third, while at higher levels, pictures may be put in order to relay a sequence of events as in a story or directions to complete a task. Patterning requires forming a consistent arrangement of materials once the pattern is started. Below are examples with age-appropriate materials.

### *Preschool/Primary*

*SP1. In this task, foam shapes of stars and hands are used to complete the sequence. The pattern is blue star, blue hand, yellow star. To complete the sequence, the next item to be put in place is the yellow hand.*

*SP2. This task is similar to SP1, but uses foam stars of different sizes to complete the ABC pattern by size in different colors. The pattern here is large green star, medium green star, small green star, large orange star, and medium orange star. The next item would be a small orange star.*

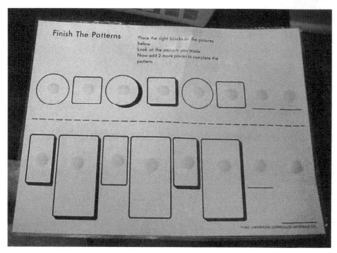

*SP3. This is a blank template (http://www. lakeshorelearning.com) for a sequencing task to be completed with matching visuals. On the top row, the pattern is circle, square, circle, square, so the next item would be circle. On the bottom row, the pattern is small rectangle, large rectangle, small rectangle, large rectangle, so the next item is small rectangle.*

SP4. This Carson-Dellosa (www.carsondellosa.com/) folder requires putting items in order by size: small, medium, and large. In structured work, the tasks should have been mastered and be visually clear so directions are not necessary.

SP5. (Below) This file folder, made from Patterns for Manipulatives (Edupress, 1995; available through major online bookstores), requires putting each set of pictures in order to tell a story. The pictures may be stored in a separate container that is placed with the folder in a bin or in a plastic bag attached to the back of the folder.

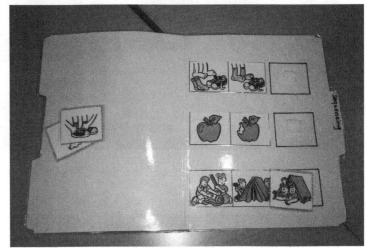

## Intermediate/Secondary/Adult

SP6. This teacher used pictures of a girl engaged in a daily routine of brushing her hair. The pictures are to be placed in order to show the steps of the routine. The task is familiar to the student, so no directions are needed.

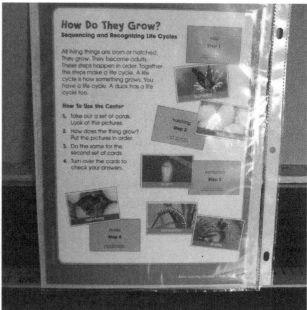

*SP7. This task requires putting pictures in order of the birth cycle for a bird hatching from an egg and a butterfly from a cocoon.*

*SP8. This shelf is set up so the videos can be ordered by either the Dewey Decimal System (as they would in a library) or in alphabetical order. Each video tape is marked with a Dewey decimal system number as well as a letter for the beginning of the title. The task is to put the videos on the shelf in the order the student or employee was previously taught.*

## Cross-Listing Tasks by Age/Developmental Level for Sequencing/Patterning Tasks

| Category | Preschool/Primary | Intermediate/Secondary/Adult |
|---|---|---|
| Sequencing/Patterning | SP1, SP2, SP3, SP4, SP5, SP6 | SP5, SP6, SP7, SP8, C5 |

## Fine Motor (FM)

Fine-motor tasks require manipulation of small pieces to build hand and finger strength and dexterity. A variety of fine-motor skills can also be practiced within tasks to strengthen eye-hand coordination and motor strength. All of the tasks listed below are ones that individuals would be familiar with and understand how to complete, so limited directions or cues are necessary.

### *Preschool/Primary*

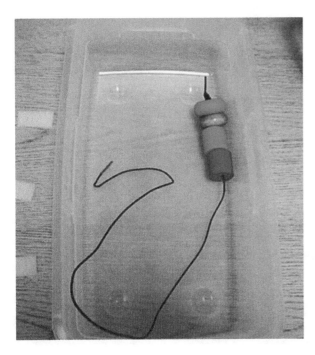

FM1. This preschool task requires lacing beads in any order to practice fine-motor skills. The picture shows the task completed. The child gets the task with the beads off the string and is familiar enough with the task to know to string them.

FM2. This task consists of a set of lacing cards. The child puts the laces through the holes to outline the object in the picture.

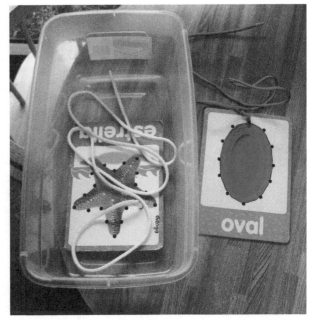

FM3. This task requires using tongs to put pom-pom balls into a muffin pan. It reinforces 1:1 correspondence (1 ball per opening) and tool use (through the use of the tongs). Typically, the pom poms would be placed on the left side of the muffin pan so the task could be completed from left to right.

FM4. Placing pegs in a pegboard is a common type of task for strengthening fine-motor skills. This would be an appropriate task for a child in early-elementary grades but would not be appropriate for older individuals, who should be working on more age-appropriate tasks.

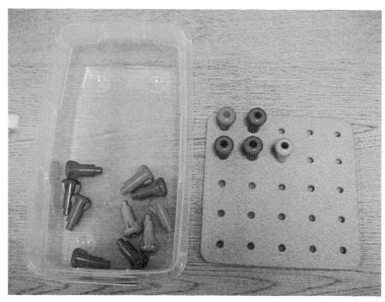

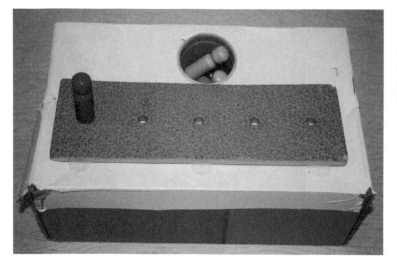

FM5. Similar to the pegboard, this task is more self-contained, requiring placing pegs in the pegboard, which is attached to the task box.

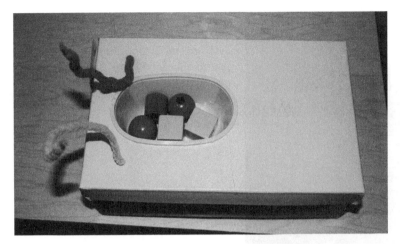

FM6. This task requires both sorting by color and stringing beads on pipe cleaners. The yellow beads have to be put on the yellow pipe cleaner and the red beads on the red pipe cleaner. The task is self-contained in a shoebox with a plastic margarine container to hold the beads. The task can be turned around so the student works from left to right (beads on the left; pipe cleaners on the right).

FM7. This task requires assembling a line of Unifix® cubes (available at major educational supply stores) in a specific order to match the picture. The complexity of the task may be easily increased. Once it has been mastered at this level, a sequence is completed without visual cues.

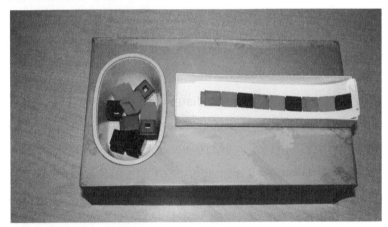

FM8. A student completing this task would practice cutting along a line to maintain cutting skills mastered during structured work.

*FM9. Puzzles are commonly used in structured work systems to match and assemble materials. This puzzle improves fine-motor skills as the student puts the pieces into the foam-based frame.*

## *Intermediate/Secondary/Adult*

Fine-motor tasks for intermediate and secondary students and adults are typically embedded into the work itself, such as packaging and assembly and disassembly tasks, which are described later. For instance, the task in FM10 would typically be classified as assembly for older students and adults, even though it also addresses fine-motor skills.

*FM10. Students or employees must assemble the bolt with the washer and the nut into one item and place it in the bin on the right. This requires not only assembling items but also practicing the fine-motor skills needed to complete this type of construction task.*

### Cross-Listing of Tasks by Age/Developmental Level for Fine-Motor Tasks

| Category | Preschool/Primary | Intermediate/Secondary/Adult |
|---|---|---|
| Fine-Motor | PI3, PI4, PI6, PI10, PI11, PI12, PI13, PI16, PI15, PI20, M4, FM1, FM2, FM3, FM4, FM5, FM6, FM7, FM8, FM9, AD6, P1 | PI6, PI15, PI17, PI20, PI21, FM10, AD12, AD13, AD14, AD16, AD17, P12, P13, P14 |

## Prereading/Reading/Functional Reading (R)

Regardless of age, everybody needs to practice using reading skills in a variety of contexts. Young children may be working on prereading skills such as matching and identifying letters, whereas adults may be working on reading directions to complete a task on the job.

A structured work system can be a good way to practice (pre)reading skills in a variety of forms. As with all the examples of tasks, the worker must be familiar with the task and have mastered it before he is asked to do it in a work system. Consequently, there is limited need for further directions, and the tasks should be self-explanatory.

### *Preschool/Primary*

*R1. This task requires matching letters in a file folder activity. In making the task, care should be taken to ensure that students match letters and not colors. The letters may be stored in a plastic bag attached to the back of the folder.*

*R2. This Carson-Dellosa (www. carsondellosa.com/) file-folder activity requires matching lowercase letters to uppercase letters. When coloring the items on the folder, care must be taken to ensure that students are not just matching by color.*

R3. This task requires matching the letters of one's name. The box at the top above the name typically has a picture of the student. The letters could be laminated cards or letter tiles found in school supply stores.

R4. To read this story, the student finds the relevant pictures to match to each part of the story.

R5. This file-folder activity requires identifying words that begin with "P." Note the use of the colored library pocket to store the pictures – these can be bought at school supply stores.

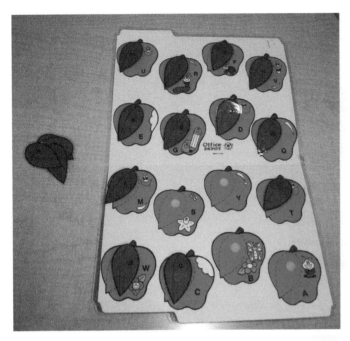

R6. This Carson-Dellosa (www.carsondellosa.com/) file-folder activity requires matching lowercase letters on the leaves to uppercase letters on the apples. Leaves that have not been matched are on the left; they may be placed in a bin for storing and presenting the task.

R7. This task requires matching pictures to words to demonstrate comprehension. The student takes the object and places it on Velcro® next to the corresponding word.

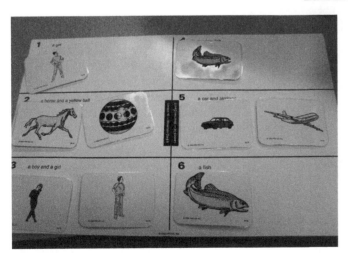

R8. This task uses the picture-matching component of the Edmark Reading Series Level 1 and 2 (http://www.proedinc.com). The student follows directions to identify pictures for phrases she has read. For example, on the bottom left, number 3 says "a boy and a girl." The student has to place the corresponding pictures of boy and girl in the space, as illustrated.

*R9. This file-folder activity requires matching phrases to pictures.*

## Intermediate/Secondary/Adult

*R10. This activity reinforces skills taught using the Edmark Functional Word Series (http://www. proedinc.com) curriculum. The task aims to generalize skills to different pictures and involves placing words of different typefaces in the pocket with the corresponding picture. The task was developed using word-processing software with different fonts and clip art found online.*

*R11. This task involves matching words in different fonts from the Edmark Functional Word Series (http://www.proedinc.com) – restaurant words – to corresponding photos. The words were printed from standard word processing software and the pictures were found online.*

*R12. This task uses clip art pictures to generalize words from the safety unit of the Edmark Functional Word series (http://www.proedinc.com). The student must take safety words learned in the Edmark Functional Word Series and printed on multiple cards in different fonts and match the written words to the corresponding picture (found online).*

*R13. This notebook task involves reading coupons and matching them to ads for the same products.*

*R14. Participants who can write answer questions about product packaging for food and health items, such as this example with a box of chicken patties. For somebody who is unable to write, the words could be available on cards in a word bank with Velcro® so they can be attached, as appropriate, to match the answers to the questions. Information can include nutritional facts, cooking directions, or recipes found on the product.*

## Cross-Listing of Tasks by Age/Developmental Level for Reading

| Category | Preschool/Primary | Intermediate/Secondary/Adult |
|---|---|---|
| Reading | M8, R1, R2, R3, R4, R5, R6, R7, R8, R9 | M8, R10, R11, R12, R13, R14, C5, C6 |

## Math (MA)

As with reading, math skills can be taught in a variety of media to individuals of all ages and everybody benefits from practicing math skills to maintain them over time. The activities below depict a range of math tasks for different ages and situations. All tasks and the way they are to be completed should be familiar to the individual before it is placed in a structured work system. Hence there is little need for additional instruction.

### *Preschool/Primary*

*MA1. Work tasks can be related to themes and holidays to add variety. This file folder is set up for Christmas and Hanukkah. Students have ornaments (Christmas tree) or candle flames (menorah) that are not pictured with the folder; they must match the objects to those with the corresponding number (e.g., ornament with a number 5 matches the yellow 5 in the middle of the tree).*

*MA2. This Carson-Dellosa (www.carsondellosa.com/) file-folder task requires matching numerals to written words of numbers. Care must be taken that the numerals and the words do not correspond in color, thereby detracting from the matching skill required.*

*MA3. This task requires matching pigs or other small manipulatives to numerals. It provides visual cues (the dots) to indicate how many to place on each card. The dots were created with dot stickers bought at an office supply store, put on index cards, and laminated.*

*MA4. This task requires placing a number of small manipulatives on cards with numerals. In this example, the student would put five small items on the card that says "5" and one small manipulative on the card that says "1." Velcroing® a patch to the card with the corresponding Velcro on the item ensures that the task stays together when finished.*

*MA5. For this teacher-made file-folder task, numerals must be matched to sets of fish.*

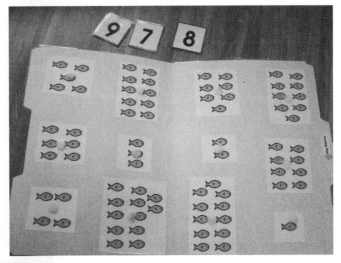

*MA6. This task requires matching numerals to sets of objects using Boardmaker® pictures.*

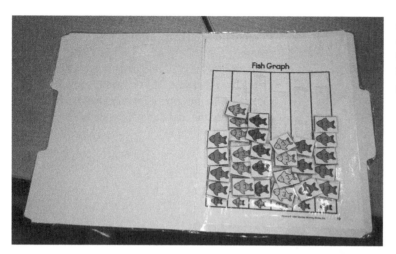

*MA7. Preschoolers completing this task must put the fish with the corresponding color to make a graph. The colored fish on the bottom of the chart are stationary and serve as a guide.*

## Intermediate/Secondary/Adult

*MA8. This task requires matching numerals to written number words. The use of page protectors/ pockets allows the instructor to switch the order and limit the number of items if needed for a specific individual.*

*MA9. This task requires filing numerals in the correct order in a file box, according to numbered index cards. The tabs on the dividers in the file box indicate ranges of numbers (e.g., 0-100; 101-200).*

MA10. This task requires using a calculator to complete simple addition problems and then placing a card with the corresponding number on top of the problem. For instance, in the upper-left corner of the card, the worker must add the numbers 1 and 5 on the calculator and place the card with 6 items and the number 6 on the Velcro dot over the 1+5 problem.

MA11. One of the difficulties with using file-folder activities for work systems with individuals with ASD is that many memorize where the pieces are to be placed without comprehending the task. This task allows the instructor to move the math problems around the folder so that the order is different each time the task is completed. The manipulatives in the bin on the right (red and blue pieces) may be used as aids for solving the problems. The manipulatives are color-coded so that the student can solve the problem in the lower-right corner by getting seven blue pieces and adding four red pieces to get the answer of 11.

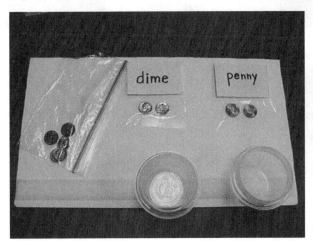

MA12 & 13. A common type of structured work task involves sorting coins. This type of task can be accomplished in a variety of ways but typically involves small containers and sets of coins that have to be sorted. Tasks can be presented with up to four types of coins to sort. In the task on the left, the sorting receptacles are fastened to a piece of foamboard with Velcro® and the corresponding coins are taped to the board above the containers using clear tape. The task on the right requires taking out the containers with the sample coins taped in the bottom and organizing the materials to sort the coins. Sorting can be done with an example of the coin or without, depending on the difficulty level needed.

MA14. For middle/secondary students or adults, being able to locate prices on a grocery flyer or menu and match them to items on a shopping list is a useful task for community activities. This task requires first finding the price on the flyer and then retrieving the price from a bank of cards and matching it to the corresponding picture of the item.

MA15. Each of these envelopes has either a price written on it or coins taped to it. The task requires matching the worth of coupons to the amount specified on the envelopes, depending upon which skill – prices or coins – the teacher wants to address and which skill the worker can demonstrate independently.

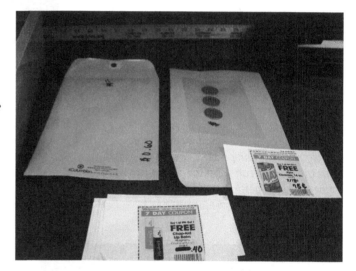

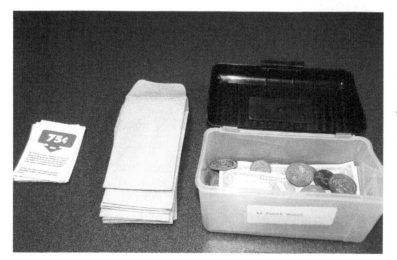

MA16. This is both an assembly and a math activity. Workers must take the cards with the price (e.g., 75¢), select the correct combination of coins and/or bills, and then place everything together in an envelope from the middle pile. The envelope goes in the bin that holds the materials (not visible here).

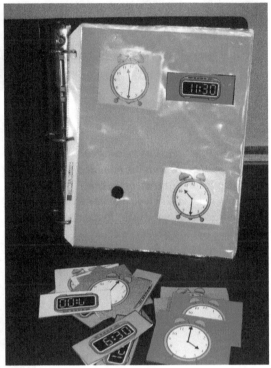

MA17. Students can complete this task with or without a Coinulator (http://www.pcieducation.com) as they match prices to cards depicting collections of coins. The Coinulator allows the student to input the value of coins by pressing realistic-looking coin buttons (e.g., pressing a quarter inputs 25 cents to the coinulator for adding to additional amounts). The use of page protectors allows the teacher to change the order of the cards periodically for students who would otherwise memorize the answers.

MA18. The task in this notebook requires matching analog clocks with digital times.

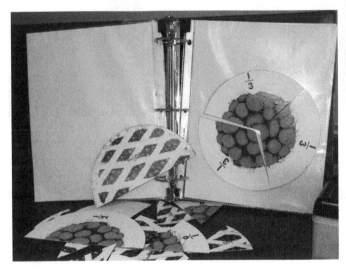

MA19. This notebook allows for sorting pieces by fractions of wholes using pictures of common items that are divided (e.g., pie, pizza).

*MA20. This task is a bit more complex. A list specifies items that must be measured out. In this case, specific amounts of rice must be measured in cups, teaspoons, or tablespoons to match the list. A similar task could be constructed to match a recipe using ingredients listed in the recipe.*

*MA21. This task requires measuring the length of items with the ruler and recording the measurements in the notebook. The worker would be familiar with this task and know what to measure; otherwise, written directions could be provided.*

## Cross-Listing of Tasks by Age/Developmental Level for Math Tasks

| Category | Preschool/Primary | Intermediate/Secondary/Adult |
|---|---|---|
| Math | MA1, MA2, MA3, MA4, MA5, MA6, MA7 | MA8, MA9, MA10, MA11, MA12, MA13, MA14, MA15, MA16, MA17, MA18, MA19, MA20, MA21, C2 |

## Writing (W)

Writing is a skill that is used on a daily basis in a variety of situations. Individuals with ASD and related disabilities often benefit from practicing these skills regularly to maintain them.  The following are examples of tasks that are put in place for individuals who are learning to write.  As noted in the secondary/adult section, most writing tasks for those workers are embedded into work activities.

### Preschool/Primary

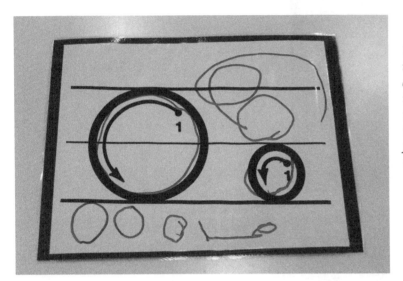

*W1. For this activity, the child is expected to copy the circle. The activity is laminated and the child uses a dry-erase marker (so the sheet can be reused). Prior to placing this task in the structured work system, the child would need to be familiar with it from explicit instruction so he would know when to stop.*

*W2. On this sheet, the child copies the alphabet letters into the box below each letter. The visual cues of the shaded boxes help keep the letters to the appropriate size.*

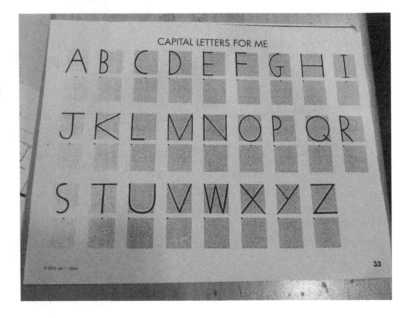

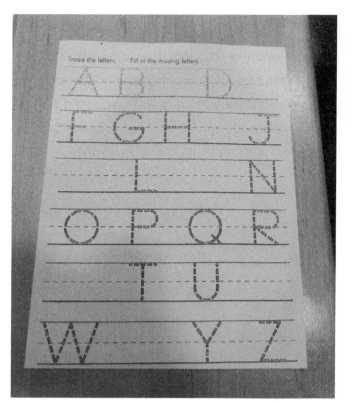

W3. In this activity, children trace some letters and also fill in the missing letters from the alphabet. This type of task allows the teacher to fade out one letter at a time and provide cues for the letters that the student can write independently. The worksheet also serves as a permanent product for data collection.

W4. On this task, the student has to write his name both in the boxes and on the lines. This allows him to practice writing his name while providing a visual cue of the number and size of the letters.

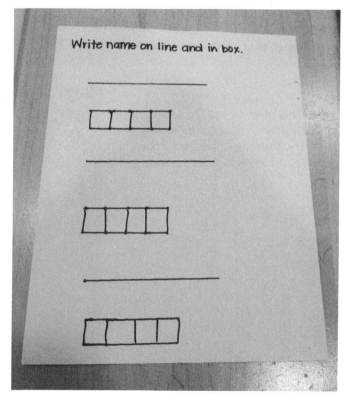

## *Intermediate/Secondary/Adult*

As with the fine-motor tasks, for intermediate and secondary students, as well as adults, writing practice typically is embedded into tasks such as clerical work. Examples may be found in the clerical work and on the cross-listing chart.

**Cross-Listing of Tasks by Age/Developmental Level for Writing Tasks**

| Category | Preschool/Primary | Intermediate/Secondary/Adult |
|----------|-------------------|------------------------------|
| **Writing** | W1, W2, W3, W4 | R14, MA21 |

## Assembly/Disassembly (AD)

It is important that participants don't learn to take apart work that they have completed. Therefore, when you are developing tasks for assembly and disassembly, be sure not to use the same materials for both types of tasks. For example, if you are using nuts and bolts as your materials, only present the task as either assembly (putting the nut on the bolt) or disassembly (unscrewing the nut from the bolt). Also, it is critical not to require that workers take their own work apart or put it together after completing it. This is demeaning to the individual's efforts and defeats the purpose of his work.

## *Preschool/Primary*

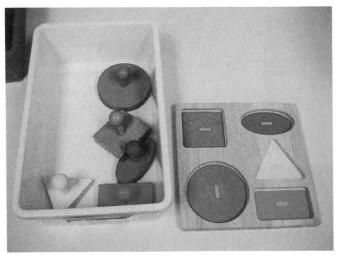

*AD1. Puzzles make good assembly tasks for young children. This puzzle has color cues in addition to shapes to help the child complete it.*

AD2. Plastic nuts and bolts (Lakeshore®, www.lakeshorelearning.com) make good assembly or disassembly materials for preschoolers and young children. They are large enough so that the task is not overwhelming, and they help match colors and shapes while completing the assembly (i.e., yellow bolts only match yellow nuts).

AD3. This task requires finding the corresponding halves of play fruits that Velcro® together to make whole fruits.

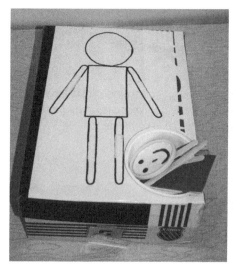

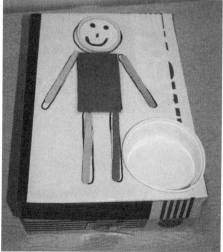

AD4. This task requires using a template to make a stick man that corresponds to the Mat Man activities in Handwriting Without Tears® (www.hwtears.com). The shapes match the common strokes of writing, and building Mat Man is part of the early childhood portion of the curriculum.

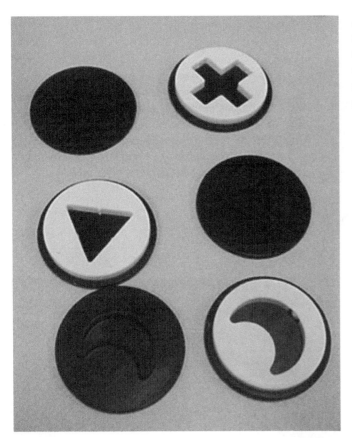

AD5. *This is a commercial game of matching Oreo shapes (Fisher-Price; http://www.fischer-price.com). Oreos are assembled by matching the inset shapes on the white side with the cut-out shape on the dark side and putting them in a bin when complete (out of sight in picture).*

AD6. *LEGOS® or Duplos® (http://www. lego.com) make good materials for assembly and disassembly tasks for young children.*

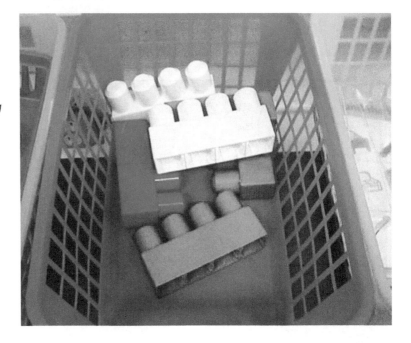

**87**

## *Intermediate/Secondary/Adult*

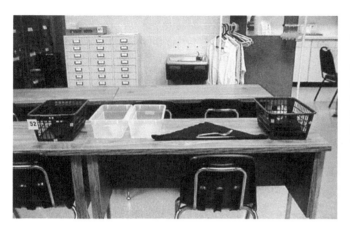

*AD7. This task requires packaging silverware by wrapping it in a napkin to prepare it for use in a restaurant. Employees take the napkin from the green basket on the left and the knife and fork from each of the two clear shoeboxes. Then they place them on the napkin, roll them up and put them in the green "finished" basket on the right.*

*AD8. This task requires putting caps on bottles as an assembly task. The task may be purchased through the Attainment Company (http://www.attainmentcompany.com) as part of its vocational work system tasks but can easily be made on your own.*

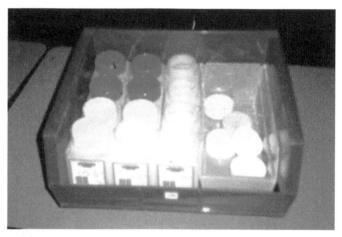

*AD9. This task requires using tools to drive nails and screw bolts into wood. This is good practice for moving on to more meaningful building jobs. The task is only appropriate for individuals who are capable of using the tools safely.*

AD10. In this basket, the task requires ability to match colors as well as motor skills to assemble the curlers since the covers only match the curlers of the same colors.

AD11. This task of folding and stacking is easily developed using washcloths. It's a good first step in practicing folding items with simple, straight lines that do not require advanced skills as clothing, for example, would.

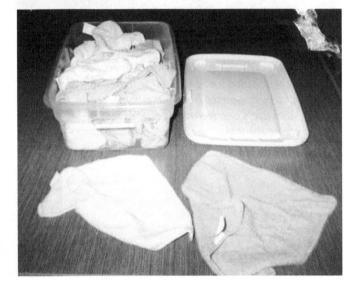

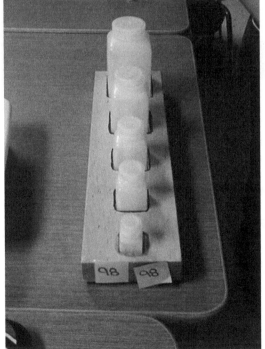

AD12. This task requires matching the top to the correct size of bottle to complete the assembly. It may be bought from the Attainment Company (http://www.attainmentcompany.com). Other options would be to save bottles in different sizes with screw-on tops, put the tops in one bin and the bottles in another.

AD13. This task involves putting erasers on top of pencils. This is a skill that might be practiced for a job in a school store that sells pencils and erasers or just to practice putting an eraser on one's own pencil.

AD14. This task requires rolling up newspapers and fastening them with a rubber band. The materials are set up to be completed from left to right. Free grocery store flyers or advertising weeklies may be used to create the task.

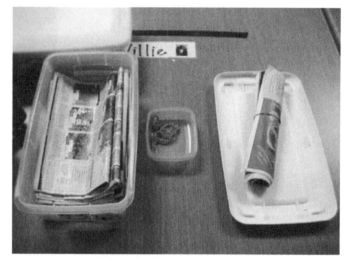

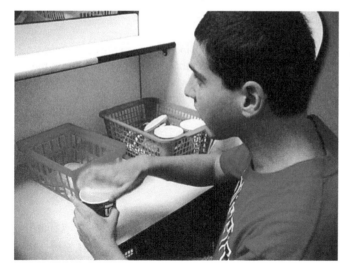

AD15. This young man is seated at a carrel to reduce distractions. He is putting tops on cups to practice the skill of fastening the top on the cup when getting soda from a fountain. He takes a cup from the left, a lid from the basket, assembles them, and places them in the basket on the right.

*AD16. A more complex assembly task, this requires placing the bins in order for putting a bolt, a washer, and a nut together. The finished product goes in bin number 4. This requires fine-motor skills in addition to sequencing and motor planning.*

*AD17. This task requires assembling the components of flashlights. To make this example more complex, the instructor used large and small flashlights. Inexpensive flashlights may be found in "dollar stores."*

### Cross-Listing of Tasks by Age/Developmental Level for Assembly/Disassembly Tasks

| Category | Preschool/Primary | Intermediate/Secondary/Adult |
|---|---|---|
| Assembly/Disassembly | AD1, AD2, AD3, AD4, AD5, AD6, TO1 | M25, FM10, AD7, AD8, AD9, AD10, AD11, AD12, AD13, AD14, AD15, AD16, AD17 |

## Packaging (P)

Packaging can be a difficult for individuals with ASD and related disabilities due to the need for motor planning. Having the opportunity to practice these skills within a structured work system allows them to become more efficient at these types of tasks, which can lead to typical jobs in vocational placements and in employment. Participants must be familiar with the packaging system and have been taught to do it before they encounter it in the structured work system; as a result, there should be limited need for directions.

## *Preschool/Primary*

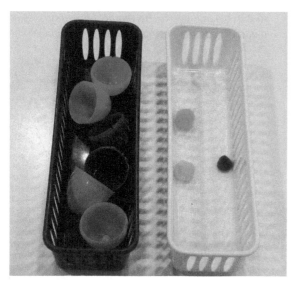

P1. This is a simple packaging task using plastic eggs. The child must find two egg halves that are the same color as the pom pom, put the pom pom in one of the egg halves and close it. The task is made easier by pairing the halves of the egg together on the left.

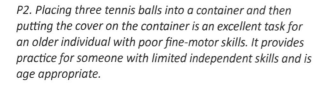

P2. Placing three tennis balls into a container and then putting the cover on the container is an excellent task for an older individual with poor fine-motor skills. It provides practice for someone with limited independent skills and is age appropriate.

P3. In this task, each toothbrush is put in a matching container. First the student takes a toothbrush and then finds the container of the same color. The student puts the toothbrush in one half of the container; the other half is locked onto the first half of the toothbrush holder and placed in a "finished" bin.

*P4. This task involves sorting cards into piles of identical cards and packaging them in matching boxes.*

*P5. This task requires sorting colored bears into containers of matching colors that are then closed for storage in the "finished" basket.*

## Intermediate/Secondary/Adult

*P6. Putting CDs on a spindle is a good introductory packaging task for somebody who needs to work on basic skills.*

*P7. This task requires sorting spoons by color, placing them inside the matching container, and then putting the lid on the container.*

*P8. This multistep task requires matching shoelaces into pairs and putting each pair into a plastic bag. The task is finished by sealing the bag.*

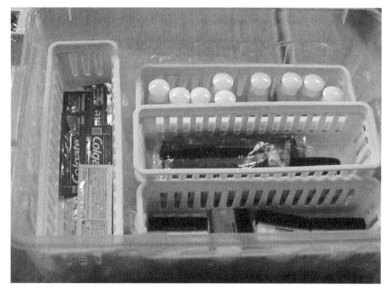

*P9. Tasks that require packaging several related items are appropriate for secondary-level students and adults as a number of jobs demand similar skills (e.g., packaging red, yellow and blue crayons in a package for distribution with placemat coloring pages in a restaurant). This task involves packaging personal hygiene articles.*

P10. Here, a toothbrush, toothpaste, and dental floss are packaged together in a plastic bag.

P11. This worker is collating yellow, white, and red pieces of paper and placing them in a vinyl pencil case.

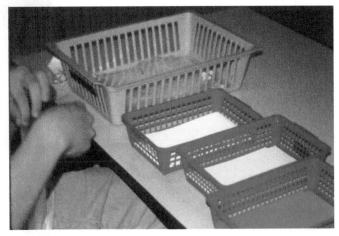

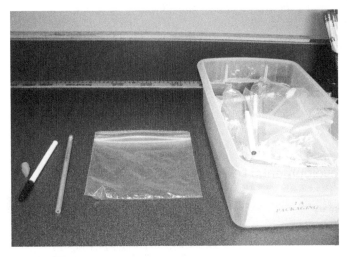

P12. This task requires getting a pen, an eraser, and a pencil from an unseen bin on the left. The worker puts the eraser on the pencil and the pencil and pen in the resealable zipper plastic bag. She zips the bag and places it in the "finished" basket to the right.

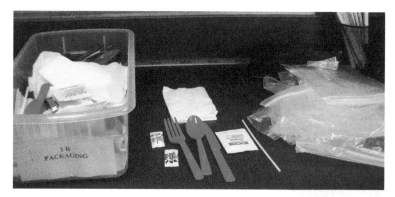

*P13. In this task, the employee assembles a set of materials for meals, including salt, pepper, plastic utensils, coffee creamer, a stir stick, and a napkin. He places it all in a resealable zipper plastic bag, sealing the package when finished. The task may be simplified with a subset of the items such as just the eating utensils.*

*P14. Here a worker practices wrapping packages using empty boxes of different sizes and sheets of tissue paper.*

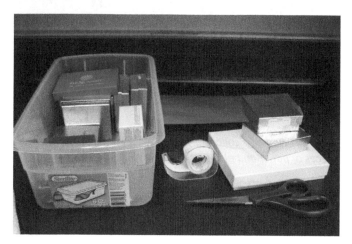

*P15. A floppy disc is placed in each vinyl case, which is subsequently closed. The completed package is put in the original plastic shoebox.*

## Cross-Listing of Tasks by Age/Developmental Level for Packaging Tasks

| Category | Preschool/Primary | Intermediate/Secondary/Adult |
|---|---|---|
| Packaging | P1, P2, P3, P4, P5 | TO2, SC25, MA15, MA16, AD7, P2, P3, P4, P6, P7, P8, P9, P10, P11, P12, P13, P14, P15 |

## Clerical (C)

Just as fine-motor tasks are generally limited to preschool/primary students as a category, clerical and other vocational tasks are limited to secondary students and adults who are working on independent tasks for job sites.

### *Intermediate/Secondary/Adult*

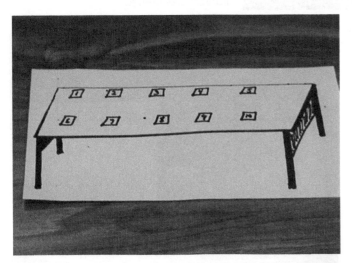

*C1. This is a template or layout for counting out 10 copies of a handout and paper-clipping them together. This is a useful school job for handling handouts and letters that have to be distributed to each classroom.*

*C2. This employee is using a template to count out 10 copies of a handout.*

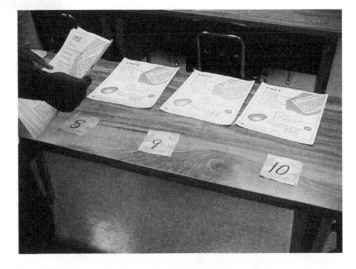

*C3. This picture demonstrates the progression of the complexity of filing tasks. Workers can start by filing according to matching stickers to begin to understand the concept of putting the cards behind the divider (like the picture filing on the far left). They can move to filing by letter (center), then to filing by word (right), and later to filing by more complex information such as mail by addresses or names.*

*C4. A file box has dividers of different colors so that pictures of objects can be sorted by color. The picture is to be placed behind the divider of the identical color.*

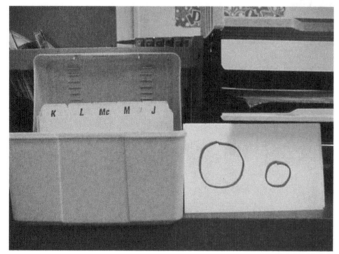

*C5. This filing task requires placing a letter behind the appropriate divider. This is an easier matching task because of the limited information included on the card than the file boxes shown above. Uppercase and lowercase letters are used to introduce the worker to having to attend to more than one letter on a card.*

*C6. This collating task is accompanied by written directions for somebody who is able to read. The worker gets a folder, puts in the papers from the boxes labeled 1 to 6, closes the folder, and puts it in the "finished" basket.*

*C7. This collating task requires simply putting a letter in a matching mailbox to practice distributing mail.*

## Cross-Listing of Tasks by Age/Developmental Level for Clerical Tasks

| Category | Preschool/Primary | Intermediate/Secondary/Adult |
|---|---|---|
| Clerical | N/A | MA9, AD13, P11, C1, C2, C3, C4, C5, C6, C7, C8 |

# HOW TO TEACH THE SYSTEM

The focus of teaching the work system should be on teaching how to complete a series of tasks in a prescribed order. In the beginning, a worker must be able to complete at least one task independently outside the system. This task could be as simple as putting two blocks in a container or taking two clothespins off the rim of a coffee can. The key is that the task must be completed without any assistance.

### Revisiting Joey, Ben, and Shandra

#### Joey

Joey, the 4-year-old child described in the introduction (see page 1), had significant difficulty completing any tasks independently in the classroom. The first step in a work system for Joey was for him to learn to independently put two blocks in a hole in the top of a shoebox. When he was able to do this with no assistance, it was time to start a more formal work system.

Joey's work system began as one shoebox on a table in front of his chair, with a "finished"

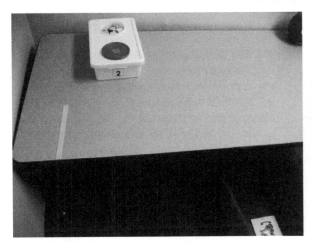

basket on the right of the table on the floor. Joey was not yet at a stage where he could manage adding a schedule to the system. Completing one task and putting it in the "finished" basket was enough for him.

*TS1. Since Joey is just learning to do work independently, he is not expected to follow a schedule of work tasks. His one basket is set out in front of him. When he completes that one task, he puts it in the "finished" basket and is then done.*

To teach Joey the system, his teacher stood behind his chair at the table and gestured toward the basket. When Joey didn't respond, she took his hand and put it on the basket. Joey pulled the basket toward him and stopped. His teacher pointed to the blocks he had to put into the hole. He picked up the first block and put it in the hole of the shoebox and then did the same with the second. Then he stopped and tried to get up. His teacher now moved closer in behind him and pointed to the box and the finished basket in order. Joey continued to try to stand up so she used hand-over-hand assistance to help him take the completed workbasket and put it in the finished basket. When he had done so, she gave him a reinforcing toy to play with for a few moments.

The next time Joey went to the structured work area, his teacher stood a little farther behind him and tried to use less prompting than the last time. She still provided the highly preferred toy after he completed the work to reinforce the use of the system. Before long, she was able to stand outside the area and watch as Joey completed the one task independently and put it away in the finished box on his own. At that point, Joey was ready to move to the next expansion of the system by completing two baskets or adding a schedule.

## Ben

The paraprofessional who supported Ben (see page 1) in the general education classroom had been struggling because he needed so much support and assistance to complete work that he could do independently in the resource class. To increase Ben's independence within the general education environment, his teacher instituted a structured work system for him to use to complete work he had mastered in the resource room. Because most of the work that Ben does in this classroom consists of paper-and-pencil tasks, his teacher planned to use a notebook or pocket folder system; the work that is to be completed will be on the left and the finished product goes in the pocket to the right.

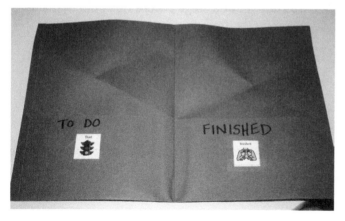

*TS2. This file folder for worksheet assignments has visual cues for work that needs to be done and work that is completed. The principle of working from left to right is being followed. (A reinforcer may be placed under the papers of the "To Do" pocket to provide immediate reinforcement upon completion of the work.)*

To teach Ben to use the system effectively, his paraprofessional stayed close to his desk the first time he used it. She was careful not to talk to him about the work so that he would not wait for her to tell him what to do. Instead, if he got stuck, she moved closer and pointed to the next step. Usually this was enough for Ben to understand what had to be done next. All of the work that he was to complete within the system was work that he could do independently in the resource room, but he tended to look for more assistance in other places. Whenever Ben looked to the paraprofessional for assistance or guidance, she silently pointed toward the work.

When he showed her his finished work, rather than putting it in the folder, she pointed to the "finished" side of the folder. When Ben finished his work and had put it in the "finished" pocket, he brought the folder to his teacher's desk and was given "choice time" to engage in a preferred activity until the rest of the class had completed their seatwork. Throughout the first week, as Ben became more independent at completing the set of tasks in his folder, the paraprofessional made sure that she moved farther away from him to fade her presence and not become a prompt for him to work. By the end of the first week, Ben was completing his assigned tasks independently and putting the folder of completed work on his teacher's desk.

## Shandra

Shandra's job coach wanted to use a structured work system to have Shandra (see page 1) complete work on the job site by herself so that she would need less supervision over time and have more opportunities for community employment. One of Shandra's jobs was to assemble brochure holders. To help her with this job, the job coach set up the work tasks with the steps presented left to right and top to bottom. She used visual schedules with photographs of each step of the task to demonstrate to Shandra how to complete each step. When Shandra finished the brochure holder, she put it in front of her work area so that her supervisor could check the quality of her work.

*TS3. A task analysis, which entails breaking down a complex or multistep task into its components, of the job using large photographs allows Shandra to assemble the brochure stands independently.*

When the job coach first introduced the new system to Shandra, she stood behind her at the table. She set the materials that Shandra would need to complete the task on the left of the table and used nonverbal prompts of pointing and hand-over-hand assistance to help Shandra complete the task according to the visual schedule. After the first holder was constructed and put in the "finished" area, the job coach stepped back and only used pointing to help Shandra pick up the material to start the task and place it in the finished area. When she looked for assistance after that, the job coach would first try a gesture from a distance before coming over to help Shandra complete a step. Within a week, Shandra could independently assemble the brochure holders assigned to her and no longer needed assistance for this task. The job coach went on to structure other tasks in Shandra's work assignments in a similar way to help her become more independent throughout the day.

## General Guidelines for Setting up Structured Work Systems

The National Professional Development Center on Autism Spectrum Disorders (2008) has outlined the steps that teachers/practitioners should take to teach how to use structured work systems. Once the work area is physically set up and structured work periods are scheduled, students are transitioned into the structured work area at the appropriate time using their visual schedules.

- The teacher stands behind the student during work sessions to provide prompts if needed. One instructor/practitioner may eventually be able to prompt two or more students, but when somebody is first learning the structured work system, he or she may need individual teaching sessions.

- The teacher/practitioner provides the least intrusive prompts possible; prompts should be nonverbal to the greatest extent possible. This is extremely important because verbal prompts are the most difficult to fade. Physical guidance, gesturing, and pointing are the preferred method of prompting structured work. The prompts should support the individual's attempt to use the components of the work system, including following the task schedule, getting the materials, and using the finished box.

- Prompts are faded as soon as the individual is able to complete the step or component. The teacher/practitioner's role becomes one of supervising instead of prompting, and then of reviewing the work completed to make sure it is done correctly. This becomes extremely important as the individual gets older and is completing work that will translate into employment tasks. The teacher should then provide feedback to let the individual know how he has done (NPD, 2008).

- Once the work is completed, the teacher/practitioner makes sure that the individual is able to determine what comes next. This may include providing a reinforcer, prompting the individual to check his schedule for the next activity, or guiding him to the break area.
- The teacher/practitioner checks the work to determine whether it was done correctly and whether any of the skills need to be reviewed in direct instruction. If the individual was not able to complete a task correctly, it is removed from the structured work area until retaught (NPD, 2008).

Often it is helpful to post goals as a reminder to all of the staff in the structured work area. The following are examples of such reminders and sample posters.

## Independent Work Skills

- Staying within an area
- Increase attention to task
- Work independently
- Follow visual system
- Complete what was started
- Practice acquired skills
- NO verbal prompts
- Child works without help

*TS4. This is a poster from a parent-child program to remind the staff and the families of what they are working towards with the structured work systems.*

*TS5. This is a posting on the work table to remind staff of how the systems work and what they are to do (e.g., use minimal verbal prompts).*

✓ Tasks in workbaskets must be mastered tasks.
✓ Work from left to right and top to bottom.
✓ Finished work in "finished" basket.
✓ Do not allow student to take work apart.
✓ Provide physical/gestural prompts when needed, then fade.
✓ Keep verbal prompts to a minimum.
✓ Block aggression.
✓ Do not allow student to escape task.

*TS6. Visual cues or written directions are often posted near the work area to remind the staff to use nonverbal prompting and where students are to sit.*

---

**Sample Poster**

**Reminders for Independent Work**

❖ Tasks in workbaskets must be mastered tasks.

❖ Students work from left to right and top to bottom.

❖ The schedule should always reflect "what's next" when the system is done.

❖ Finished work is put in the "finished" basket.

❖ Do not allow students to take work apart.

❖ Do not take work apart in front of students.

❖ Provide physical/gestural prompts when needed, then fade.

❖ Use nonverbal prompts only.

---

## Expanding the System

As individuals with ASD develop their abilities to complete a variety of tasks while following a structured schedule, it is important to increase the difficulty and complexity of the system so that skills continue to improve and expand. This can be done in several ways, including the following:

- Increase the number of baskets that are completed, moving from one to two, three and four baskets.
- Add more materials to each basket. That will build endurance and increase the amount of time the individual is able to work independently.
- Incorporate a task schedule that the worker must follow. The schedule can be represented by a variety of symbols that must be matched to the task containers.
- Use letters or numbers that are not in order on the schedule.
- Store the work tasks in another area of the room and have a "finished" area away from the work table. The worker must then leave the work table to get his tasks and to put them away when done. This requires self-control and direction, and mastery will allow for more independence and success in employment.
- Think about other ways to use the system to build skills once workers are using a multitask, structured work schedule. Suggestions include the following:
  - Set up tasks that necessitate two individuals working together to complete them, like setting up a mini-assembly line in which each person completes a different step of the process.
  - Embed the need to send messages to adults/supervisors into the structured work system. Individuals with ASD have difficulty initiating communication but need to be able to ask for help or a break during work. This can be accomplished by sabotaging the task (e.g., not providing all of the material needed to complete a task).

*TS7. This work area provides communication visuals along the bottom of the table to help the student request assistance, ask for a break, or ask for attention – common functions of challenging behaviors for students using this system. This type of support also allows the staff to "sabotage" the activities so that students who could do the system independently learn to ask for help when needed materials are missing.*

# COLLECTING DATA

As for all other aspects of training, it is important to collect data during structured work. For example, data allow a teacher/practitioner or supervisor to keep track of the worker's performance as a means of evaluating the effectiveness of the teaching procedures that are being used. A tracking sheet lets all staff know what skills each participant is working on at a given time so that anyone in the room can set up the structured work area. Performance data also allow the individual to provide information to potential employers about the type of work tasks she is proficient at completing. To that end, developing a portfolio showing work at a variety of tasks is an effective way to portray a person's skills.

The tasks that are included in structured work should be tracked for each participant to ensure that they have been mastered. They should be rotated frequently to ensure that a variety of skills are practiced for maintenance of previously mastered tasks. It is also important to take data on performance of the steps in the structured work routine. Several data collection forms have been developed for this purpose.

The first data sheet, Independent Work Task Analysis Data Sheet on page 110, is based on a task analysis of the steps in completing a three-basket work system with a work schedule and the tasks placed on the table in front of the individual. The form also provides a space to record aspects of the work such as type of prompts used and duration (amount) of time it takes for the worker to complete the work from beginning to end. "Sd" stands for "discriminative stimulus," an applied behavior analysis term that refers to the directions given to the student.

The data sheet lists 29 steps. The instructor records the steps on which the individual needs prompting and those he has completed independently. Data are taken at least weekly. The data sheet is self-graphing so that it is easy to determine whether the individual is becoming more independent. The data collector circles the total number of independent steps for each day when data are collected. By connecting those points, which represent the number of steps the person could do independently, a graph is created showing whether there is progress being made. In the example on page 110, the data are shown for Joey at a point in his program where he is able to complete three tasks instead of the one shown earlier (see pages 101-102).

# Skill Acquisition Program
## *INDEPENDENT WORK TASK ANALYSIS DATA SHEET*

| SKILL: Work Basket System | STUDENT'S NAME: Joey Miller |
|---|---|
| AREA: Cognitive/Learning | TARGET BEHAVIOR: Student will complete a set of work baskets when given the Sd. |
| Sd: "Do your work," "work time" or "basket time" | PREREQUISITES: Student can perform tasks in baskets independently. |
| PRIMARY INSTRUCTOR: | PROCEDURAL STEPS: Student is prompted through basket activities with trainer using prompts. Prompts are gradually faded out. |

| DATE: | 12/12/11 | 12/13/11 | 12/15/11 | | | | | |
|---|---|---|---|---|---|---|---|---|
| TIME: | 10:15 am | 10:15 am | 10:15 am | | | | | |
| PROMPTS: | P, G | P, G | G | | | | | |
| DURATION: | 10 mins | 9 mins | 10 mins | | | | | |
| BASKET ITEMS: | A B C | C B A | B A C | | | | | |
| 29. Occupies time appropriately after completing baskets. | 29 | 29 | 29 | 29 | 29 | 29 | 29 | 29 |
| 28. Asks for help if materials are missing. | 28 | 28 | 28 | 28 | 28 | 28 | 28 | 28 |
| 27. Accesses reinforcer. | 27 | 27 | 27 | 27 | 27 | 27 | 27 | 27 |
| 26. Puts completed basket into "finished" basket or area. | 26 | (26) | 26 | 26 | 26 | 26 | 26 | 26 |
| 25. Puts activity back into basket. | 25 | 25 | 25 | 25 | 25 | 25 | 25 | 25 |
| 24. Completes activity. | 24 | 24 | (24) | 24 | 24 | 24 | 24 | 24 |
| 23. Sets up activity. | 23 | 23 | 23 | 23 | 23 | 23 | 23 | 23 |
| 22. Takes activity out of basket. | 22 | 22 | 22 | 22 | 22 | 22 | 22 | 22 |
| 21. Places third basket in front of self. | 21 | 21 | 21 | 21 | 21 | 21 | 21 | 21 |
| 20. Matches third shape. | 20 | 20 | 20 | 20 | 20 | 20 | 20 | 20 |
| 19. Pulls off third shape. | (19) | 19 | 19 | 19 | 19 | 19 | 19 | 19 |
| 18. Puts completed basket into "finished" basket or area. | 18 | 18 | 18 | 18 | 18 | 18 | 18 | 18 |
| 17. Puts activity back into basket. | 17 | 17 | 17 | 17 | 17 | 17 | 17 | 17 |
| 16. Completes activity. | 16 | 16 | 16 | 16 | 16 | 16 | 16 | 16 |
| 15. Sets up activity. | 15 | 15 | 15 | 15 | 15 | 15 | 15 | 15 |
| 14. Takes activity out of basket. | 14 | 14 | 14 | 14 | 14 | 14 | 14 | 14 |
| 13. Places second basket in front of self. | 13 | 13 | 13 | 13 | 13 | 13 | 13 | 13 |
| 12. Matches second shape. | 12 | 12 | 12 | 12 | 12 | 12 | 12 | 12 |
| 11. Pulls off second shape. | 11 | 11 | 11 | 11 | 11 | 11 | 11 | 11 |
| 10. Puts completed basket into "finished" basket or area. | 10 | 10 | 10 | 10 | 10 | 10 | 10 | 10 |
| 9. Puts activity back into basket. | 9 | 9 | 9 | 9 | 9 | 9 | 9 | 9 |
| 8. Completes activity. | 8 | 8 | 8 | 8 | 8 | 8 | 8 | 8 |
| 7. Sets up activity. | 7 | 7 | 7 | 7 | 7 | 7 | 7 | 7 |
| 6. Takes activity out of basket. | 6 | 6 | 6 | 6 | 6 | 6 | 6 | 6 |
| 5. Places first basket in front of self. | 5 | 5 | 5 | 5 | 5 | 5 | 5 | 5 |
| 4. Matches first shape. | 4 | 4 | 4 | 4 | 4 | 4 | 4 | 4 |
| 3. Pulls off first shape. | 3 | 3 | 3 | 3 | 3 | 3 | 3 | 3 |
| 2. Sits in chair. | 2 | 2 | 2 | 2 | 2 | 2 | 2 | 2 |
| 1. Walks to basket area. | 1 | 1 | 1 | 1 | 1 | 1 | 1 | 1 |
| STAFF INITIALS: | SK | SK | SK | | | | | |
| LEVEL OF MASTERY: | | | | | | | | |

| Scoring Code: | Prompts | Comments/Observations: |
|---|---|---|
| / Correct | P-Physical | 12/ 12/ 11   Needed help getting started |
| - Prompted | G-Gestural | |
| X Incorrect | S-Visual | 12/ 13/ 11   Needed help getting started |
| O Circle total | V-Visual prompt from a distance | |
| correct | 0-Does not perform step | 12/ 16/ 11   Needed help getting started |

| Criterion for Mastery: | Basket Items: | | |
|---|---|---|---|
| | A. Put in - chips   C. Transfer Material   F. | I. | |
| | B. Pull apart beads   D.   G. | J. | |
| | E.   H. | K. | |

A second data sheet, Structured Work Systems Data Sheet, includes the elements of the work and system for the individual worker. The top half of the form includes information about the types of tasks, how they are organized, the type of work system used, the physical environment of the work area, and the "what comes next." The bottom half of the form includes a daily data space for one week in which the teacher/practitioner circles the most intrusive prompt used that day. It is suggested that data be recorded every day with this system due to the ease of use.

## Structured Work Systems Data Sheet

Worker's Name: Shandra Hines          Date: 12/12/12

Instructor: Ms. Smith _____          _____

### System Design

| Tasks | Matching<br>Sorting<br>(Assembly/disassembly)<br>Packaging<br>Sequencing<br>(Office)<br>Pre/func academics | Jigs<br>(Model)<br>Picture dictionary<br>Picture/written directions | |
|---|---|---|---|
| Work System | Number of Tasks _3_<br><br>Work period 30 minutes<br>2 Work periods/day | Tasks on work surface<br>Tasks next to work area<br>(Tasks in separate area)<br>"Finished" basket<br>("Finished" area) | No system<br>Match color, shape, object,<br>numbers, letters<br>(List color) shape, object,<br>(numbers) letters |
| Environment | Enclosed cubby<br>At desk<br>Common area | Self-contained class<br>Regular education<br>(Vocational Lab) | |
| What Comes Next | Reinforcer at work area<br>Token<br>(Choice time)<br>Check schedule<br>Activity at work area | | |

### Data for the Week of   12/12/2012

| Monday | Tuesday | Wednesday | Thursday | Friday |
|---|---|---|---|---|
| Independent | Independent | Independent | Independent | (Independent) |
| Visual Cue | Visual Cue | Visual Cue | Visual Cue | Visual Cue |
| (Gestural Prompt) | (Gestural Prompt) | Gestural Prompt | (Gestural Prompt) | Gestural Prompt |
| Physical Prompt | Physical Prompt | (Physical Prompt) | Physical Prompt | Physical Prompt |
| Verbal Prompt<br>(Last Resort) | Verbal Prompt<br>(Last Resort) | Verbal Prompt<br>(Last Resort) | Verbal Prompt<br>(Last Resort) | Verbal Prompt<br>(Last Resort) |

12/14/12 Not feeling well.

A third data collection option, Work System Data Sheet, is a form that was modified from Division TEACCH (www.teacch.com). It is designed to take data during one work session and includes space for up to four different tasks in the system. It is easy to use, as the teacher/instructor only circles the type of prompt, if any, needed to complete each of the tasks. The focus is on support for approaching, beginning, and completing the task, and doing what comes next. This sheet should be completed at least once a week.

## Work System Data Sheet (adapted from TEACCH)

**Student's Name:** Ben Jones      **Date:** 12/12/12      **Work System:** Match numbers

### Information Provided

__✓__ What work?      __✓__ How much work?      __✓__ When finished?      __✓__ What next?

|  | Checks Schedule | Begins Task | Completes Task | Puts in Finished area |
|---|---|---|---|---|
| **Task #1** | (Independent) | (Independent) | (Independent) | Independent |
|  | Visual | Visual | Visual | Visual |
|  | (Gestural) | Gestural | Gestural | (Gestural) |
|  | Physical | Physical | Physical | Physical |
|  | 0 | 0 | 0 | 0 |
| **Task #2** | (Independent) | (Independent) | (Independent) | (Independent) |
|  | Visual | Visual | Visual | Visual |
|  | Gestural | Gestural | Gestural | Gestural |
|  | Physical | Physical | Physical | Physical |
|  | 0 | 0 | 0 | 0 |
| **Task #3** | (Independent) | (Independent) | (Independent) | (Independent) |
|  | Visual | Visual | Visual | Visual |
|  | Gestural | Gestural | Gestural | Gestural |
|  | Physical | Physical | Physical | Physical |
|  | 0 | 0 | 0 | 0 |
| **Task #4** | Independent | Independent | Independent | Independent |
|  | Visual | Visual | Visual | Visual |
|  | Gestural | Gestural | Gestural | Gestural |
|  | Physical | Physical | Physical | Physical |
|  | 0 | 0 | 0 | 0 |

Adapted with permission from Susan Boswell, TEACCH Autism Program. Copyright 2011.

## Teaching With Fidelity

The evidence base of an educational practice is only as good as the degree to which it is implemented with fidelity. Failure to implement a strategy accurately reduces its effectiveness. One way to ensure fidelity with structured work systems is to do periodic observations of their use. The National Professional Development Center on Autism Spectrum Disorders (2008) has developed an extensive checklist for completing observations that may be found at their website, www.autismpdc.fpg.unc.edu.

Another tool, the Structured Works Systems Competency-Based Checklist, is a bit more concise, easier and quicker to use (see page 114). This checklist provides a framework for observations that may be conducted by a teacher, a principal, a special education administrator, or a job coach. In addition, it may be used by the staff member to periodically check on each other's performance to ensure that the practice remains consistent and accurate over time. For instance, a teacher and a paraprofessional could observe each other conducting structured work and subsequently give feedback and discuss any needed changes or difficulties encountered.

The Structured Work Systems Competency-Based Checklist p. 114 shows a completed checklist for a paraprofessional in Joey's classroom, who was observed by the teacher. The areas checked "no" are parts of the system they reviewed after the observation for future implementation and retraining, if necessary.

## Structured Work Systems
## Competency-Based Checklist

| Instructor: Ms. Jones | Date: 12/12/2012 |
|---|---|
| Observer: Ms. Ward | Length of Observation: 15 minutes |
| Student(s): Joey Miller | Skill/Activity Observed: Ind Work |

Check off presence of the skill in yes/no boxes. Check N/A if a given skill does not apply within this observation.

| Skills | Yes | No | N/A | Comments |
|---|---|---|---|---|
| The system tells the worker how much work needs to be done. | × | | | |
| The system tells the worker what work needs to be done. | × | | | |
| The system lets the worker know when he or she is finished. | × | | | |
| The system provides information about what happens next. | × | | | |
| All work tasks contained in the system are previously mastered. | | × | | 2nd task not ind |
| Work is individualized to the worker's functioning level. | × | | | |
| Instructor reserves praise and reinforcement for completion of the system. | × | | | |
| Completed tasks are placed in the "finished" area without being taken apart. | × | | | |
| Instructors do not reset the work in front of the worker. | | × | | |
| Instructors use only nonverbal prompts to teach the system. | | × | | |
| Instructor uses the least amount of assistance necessary to help the worker master the system. | × | | | |
| Instructor fades physical proximity to the area as the worker gains independence. | × | | | Backed away |
| Data are collected accurately on a regular schedule. | × | | | Weekly |
| Data are reviewed regularly and the tasks and system are modified based on that analysis. | | × | | |

114

# CONCLUSION

Individuals with ASD and related disorders are supported by a variety of people through-out their day, whether in general education, resource, or self-contained educational settings; work settings; transition programs; or at home. Structured work systems are one method that can be used to ensure that they develop and maintain their ability to work on their own, without assistance and prompting from adults and peers.

A wide variety of tasks can be integrated into the systems, ranging from building academic skills to practicing vocational tasks. The system itself and its pattern of working left to right and putting tasks away when completed can be used to teach good work habits as well. In addition to the benefits to the individual with ASD or other disabilities, work systems provide a time during the day when instructors are freed up to provide direct instruction to other students, managers to supervise other employees, and parents and group home staff to do other tasks around the house.

Finally, in the writers' experiences, for many individuals with ASD, the structured work time is their favorite part of the day. The predictability and sense of accomplishment that are built into the system, as well as the reinforcer that typically follows completion of the tasks, are rewarding for these individuals in the same way that many of us make a list of things to do and take a break when we have crossed off the last item. As students progress through the systems, many become able to move toward more conventional methods of managing work activities (e.g., to-do list). However, regardless of whether he or she needs the structure of the system or can move to other methods, each student can feel good when completing the system.

# FREQUENTLY ASKED QUESTIONS

**Q:** My student with ASD always finishes his tasks before the structured work period is over. What can I do to increase the time he stays in this area?

**A:** There are a number of ways to increase the amount of time it takes to complete the work. For example, the number of baskets in the system can be increased. Or for students who can complete a limited number of baskets at a given time, the amount of material included in each basket can be increased (e.g., putting two file folders in a basket instead of one or putting 10 sets of silverware in the basket for packaging instead of 5). You can also have a preferred activity at the structured work area for the student to engage in once the work is completed to keep her occupied until it is time to move to another center or activity.

**Q:** Several of my students aren't independent at doing anything. Where do I start with structured work systems?

**A:** First, you need to determine what simple tasks the student can complete on his own. Start with simple "put-in" or "pull-apart" tasks. One of the easiest tasks is to put chips in a slot of a container. If the student is able to do this independently, you can organize the materials in a basket and just put them on the table in front of him. Then prompt him to take the container with the slot and a bowl with chips out of the basket. His task is to transfer the chips from the bowl into the container. Nonverbal prompting will allow him to master this simple one-task system. When he has mastered this, add a basket with another simple, mastered task.

**Q:** My student's mother objects to him doing structured work because he can already do the tasks. How do I explain the value of this process to her?

**A:** The point of a structured work system is to build the child's skills by completing a series of previously mastered tasks. It is not to teach new tasks. Specifically, the goal is to teach the child to use a visual schedule to guide him through a series of tasks. It is also to teach him to place all of his completed work in a finished area and not disassemble work that he has completed. Students are taught to always work from left to right and top to bottom; this orientation allows them to apply a systematic way to approach work to any situation. Another goal of this activity is to build endurance so that students increase the amount of time spent on a task and the amount of work they are able to complete independently. It is also important to explain that individuals with ASD often lose skills they had previously mastered when they are not practiced regularly or reintroduced. Structured work allows the individual to practice these tasks so he does not lose skills he has gained.

**Q:** This looks too simple for my students. Why should I do this in my classroom (or work setting)?

**A:** One of the greatest advantages to scheduling structured work systems as a center rotation or activity period is that it allows the staff to provide explicit instruction to an individual student or group of students while others are working independently. In many settings, one staff member can monitor two to three students at a time in the structured work area. Simply organizing academic work into a file pocket system, such as Ben's (see page 3), can be beneficial in increasing independence. In addition, even higher functioning individuals, like Ben, have difficulty working alone or become anxious when tasks are not broken down.

**Q:** My client is distracted by other activities going on in the room. How can I arrange the structured work area to reduce distractions?

**A:** When the physical arrangement of the room is being designed, it is important to consider where to place the structured work area. It is often a good idea to put this area in a corner of the room where the person faces the wall so as not to be distracted by other activities. It is also critical that highly distracting activities, such as the computer, be placed away from the structured work area. When a person is extremely distractible, a moveable divider can be placed behind her to block visual access to other activities taking place. Another option would be to provide a study carrel as seen in picture SU8.

**Q:** I don't have enough staff in my setting to teach the structured work system initially. How can I assign staff to make sure that our clients learn how to follow the system?

**A:** When a structured work system is being introduced, it is useful to start with the most capable individual and teach her the structured work system first. Once you have one person who is able to work in this center independently, add another and teach him the system. Continue teaching the system to one person at a time. If you need to have several workers in the structured work area at a time due to schedule and supervision requirements, have the supervising paraprofessional or aide work with one worker and keep the others engaged with highly preferred items/activities that they can handle independently.

Q: My students don't stay in the structured work area. How can I make sure that they are motivated to stay in the area until the work period is over?

A: Even using a structured work system, individuals with ASD most likely need the motivation of a desired activity or item they can engage with when their work is complete. As such, the work schedule should include an indication of what will happen when the assigned tasks have been completed. This can be a visual that says, "Check your schedule," which will take the employee to his next activity; or "Take a break," which will send him to a break area of the room where he can do what he wants for the duration of the break. Other options for indicating what comes next (i.e., reinforcers) include a visual showing a book or some other visual that sends the employee to pick one of the items to use in the area, or a basket of sensory objects on the work surface that follows the sets of tasks that have to be completed. Working from left to right takes the person to that basket when all other work has been completed.

Q: My employee keeps undoing a task and putting it partway together again. How can I make sure that he learns to keep his work together?

A: When an individual starts on a job site, it is important that he does not undo work that he has completed. That will negatively affect his performance on the job. It is important that our employees learn to keep their work assembled when it is put in the finished basket or area. The individual who is monitoring the structured work area has to be vigilant in ensuring that workers keep their work together. Designating a specific spot to place finished work may help an employee complete the task, put it away, and move on.

Q: Does this mean that my students will need a work system forever? Do I want to wean them from following the work schedule?

A: It is important that individuals with ASD have systems that they can take with them and apply to new settings and tasks. The structured work system is one of those systems that can be imported to new environments to reduce anxiety and facilitate independent functioning. The system can become more sophisticated as individuals gain skills but should always be available to them. For example, some individuals may move to more sophisticated systems, such as a list of things to do, but the system should remain in place. If the individual stops being independent after introduction to a new system, it is important to go back to a simpler system.

**Q:** Does each student need to have his or her own structured work space?

**A:** Settings for students with ASD typically have centers that meet the environmental needs of a variety of activities, and it is often difficult for each student to have his own structured work area. It is useful to include structured work as part of a center rotation and have several students use the same area. Some instructors have two or three structured work tables/desks and set them up so that one is for students with very basic skills, one for students in the middle, and the third for those with more advanced skills. That way, the students can be placed at the desk that has the tasks most suitable for them. Other instructors group their students by level, so that everybody needing the most basic tasks is at structured work at the same time. In that case, it is important to organize each student's tasks so that setup between center rotations proceeds smoothly. In most situations, it is important to conduct direct instruction of new skills in a different area from structured work to avoid confusion.

**Q:** When structured work is part of a center rotation and new students need to use the space immediately after other students, it is difficult for me and my paraprofessionals to reset the systems to be ready for the next students. Is it all right if I take the work apart and reset the structured work station while the student is still sitting there?

**A:** No! Never disassemble work in front of the person who completed it. When you do that, you devalue the work, which can lead to low self-esteem and work refusal. A person inevitably thinks that his work doesn't matter when it is undone right after he has put forth his best effort to complete it. To get around this problem, have him engage in his "what's next" activity in an adjacent area where he will not notice you checking and resetting his work.

**Q:** How can I apply the strategies used in educational settings in the community or at a job site?

**A:** As students get older and more of their program moves to the community, or they move on to an adult program or paid employment, structured work systems can be implemented at those locations, too. While students are preparing for transition, staff should analyze the demands of the work environments and provide visual supports to allow students to be as independent as possible at the work site. Shandra's system provides one example (TS3).

**Q:** My students' parents tell me that their children can't do anything independently at home. Can structured work systems be used in the home environment?

**A:** Absolutely. It is easy for parents to use the same principles of organizing simple tasks or play materials to keep their children engaged while the parents are busy with household tasks. Using baskets and containers to organize the pieces needed for the tasks allows the child to see what has to be done. A "finished" basket can also be provided so the child can follow a familiar process, which also allows for easy cleanup when the time is done.

**Q:** My staff wants to praise the workers or verbally prompt them when teaching the system. Is this O.K.?

**A:** The goal for time spent in structured work should be independent performance. Therefore, staff should only provide gestural and physical cues. Such cues can be faded much more easily than verbal cues. In addition, it is important to ensure that the person is able to complete work without needing praise from the staff while he or she is working. Of course, everyone likes to receive praise so it should be given when the worker has completed his time in this area of the room.

# REFERENCES

Arick, J., Loos, L., Falco, R., & Krug, D. (2003). *The STAR program: Strategies for teaching based on autism research*. Austin, TX: PRO-ED.

Bennett, K., Reichow, B., & Wolery, M. (2011). Effects of structured teaching on the behavior of your children with disabilities. *Focus on Autism and Other Developmental Disabilities, 26*(3), 143-152.

Carnahan, C., Harte, H., Schumacher, K., Hume, K., & Borders, C. (2011). Structured Work Systems: Supporting meaningful engagement in preschool settings for children with autism spectrum disorders. *Young Exceptional Children, 14*(1), 2–16.

Dettmer, S., Simpson, R. L., Myles, B. S., & Ganz, J. B. (2000). The use of visual supports to facilitate transitions of students with autism. *Focus on Autism and Other Developmental Disabilities, 15*, 163-169.

Hume, K., & Odom, S. (2007). Effects of an individual work system on the independent functioning of students with autism. *Journal of Autism and Developmental Disorders, 37*(6), 1166-1180.

Hume, K., Plavnick, J., & Odom, S. L. (2012). Promoting task accuracy and independent in students with autism across educational setting through the use of individual work systems. *Journal of Autism and Developmental Disorders*. doi.10.1007//s10803-012-11457-4

Hume, K., & Reynolds, B. (2010). Implementing work systems across the school day: Increasing engagement in students with autism spectrum disorders. *Preventing School Failure: Alternative Education for Children and Youth, 54*(4), 228–237.

Krantz, P. J., MacDuff, M. T., & McClannahan, L. E. (1993). Programming participation in family activities for children with autism: Parents' use of photographic activity schedules. *Journal of Applied Behavior Analysis, 26*, 137-138.

MacDuff, G. S., Krantz, P., & McClannahan, L. (1993). Teaching children with autism to use photographic activity schedules: Maintenance and generalization of complex response chains. *Journal of Applied Behavior Analysis, 26*(1), 89-97.

National Autism Center (2009). *National standards report.* Author: Randolph, MA: Author.

National Professional Development Center on Autism Spectrum Disorders. (2008). *Module: Individualized work systems.* Chapel Hill, NC: The University of North Carolina, The National Professional Development Center on Autism Spectrum Disorders, Frank Porter Graham Child Development Institute.

# APPENDIX A

## Resources for Structured Work

### *Commercially Prepared Tasks*

www.attainmentcompany.com
This company offers a variety of functional assembly tasks that are appropriate for secondary-level students. They come in different sets that range from simple to more advanced.

www.hot-ideas.org
These tasks come with all the required pieces and containers but must be put together. A large number of types of tasks are available, ranging from simple put-in tasks to more complex vocational tasks for older students.

www.shoeboxtasks.com
These tasks are very simple and appropriate for young children who have few skills. They include put-in, pull-apart, transfer, stacking, and simple sorting tasks. The tasks are self-contained and are extremely durable.

### *Internet Resources for File Folder Activities*

www.amug.org/~jbpratt/education/theme/filefolders.html

www.angelfire.com/pa5/as/myprintables.html

www.childcareland.com/filefoldergames.html

www.enchantedlearning.com/filefoldergames

www.filefolder.com

www.filefolderfun.com/SearchAge.html

www.myffgames.com

www.preschoolprintables.com/filefolder/filefolder.shtml

### *Books With How-to-Make Tasks Information*

Baratta-Lorton, M. (1972). *Workjobs: Activity-centered learning for early childhood.* Boston, MA: Addison Wesley Publishing Company.

Baratta-Lorton, M. (1978). *Workjobs II: Number activities for early childhood.* Parsippany, NJ: Dale Seymour Publications.

Baratta-Lorton, M. (1995). *Mathematics their way, spiral-bound teacher guide plus blackline masters.* Parsippany, NJ: Dale Seymour Publications.

Boswell, S. (2007). *TEACCH preschool curriculum guide: A curriculum planning and monitoring guide for young children with autism and related communication disorders.* www.lulu.com

Burch, M. M. (2001). *Instant file-folder games for reading: Super-fun, super-easy reproducible games that help kids build important reading skills-independently!* Jefferson City, MO: Scholastic Professional Books.

Carson-Dellosa Publishing Company. (1990). *File folder games reading and math, grade 1.* www.carsondellosa.com/

Clarke, J. (2002). *Show box math learning centers: Forty easy-to-make, fun-to-use centers with instant reproducibles and activities that help kids practice important math skills – independently, grades 1-3.* Jefferson City, MO: Scholastic Professional Books.

Eckenrode, L., Fennel, P., & Hearsey, K. (2003). *Tasks galore: Book one.* Raleigh, NC: Tasks Galore.

Eckenrode, L., Fennel, P., & Hearsey, K. (2004). *Tasks galore: For the real world.* Raleigh, NC: Tasks Galore.

Eckenrode, L., Fennel, P., & Hearsey, K. (2005). *Tasks galore: Making groups meaningful.* Raleigh, NC: Tasks Galore.

Eckenrode, L., Fennel, P., Hearsey, K., & Reynolds, B. (2009). *Tasks galore: Let's play.* Raleigh, NC: Tasks Galore.

Hamill, L., & Dunlevy, A. (1999). *Work boxes activity book.* San Antonio, TX: PCI Education.

Henry, K. A. (2005). *How do I teach this kid?* Arlington, TX: Future Horizons.

Linton, S. B. (2009). *How to set up a work area at home for a child with autism: A manual for parents, family members, and in-home support providers.* www.autismclassroom.com

Talmage, K. L., & Dobrofsky, V. (2007). *Climbing art obstacles in autism.* Raleigh, NC: Tasks Galore.

Thomas, R., Black, M. W., & McAuliffe, M. M. (2004). *File folder activities for learning centers.* Westminster, CA: Teacher Created Resources.

Thorne, B. (2001). *Hands-on activities for exceptional students: Educational and pre-vocational activities for students with cognitive delays.* Minnetonka, MN: Peytral Publications, Inc.

Treatment and Education of Autistic and related Communication handicapped Children (TEACCH). (1992). *Independent tasks: Work activities for students with autism and other visual learners.* Chapel Hill, NC: Author.

*Articles Supporting the Evidence Base of Structured Work Systems*

Autism Internet Module. *Structured work systems.* www.autisminternetmodules.org

Bennett, K., Reichow, B., & Wolery, M. (2011). Effects of structured teaching on the behavior of young children with disabilities. *Focus on Autism and Other Developmental Disabilities, 26*(3), 143-152.

Bryan, L. C., & Gast, D. L. (2000). Teaching on-task and on-schedule behaviors to high-functioning children with autism via picture activity schedules. *Journal of Autism and Developmental Disorders, 30*(6), 553-567.

Burgess, S. (2001). *Developing independent activities for young students with autism.* Chapel Hill, NC: University of North Carolina TEACCH. Available at www.teacch.com

Carnahan, C. R., Hume, K., Clarke, L., & Borders, C. (2009). Using structured work systems to promote independence and engagement for students with autism spectrum disorders. *Teaching Exceptional Children, 41*(4), 6-14.

Durant, S. L. (1982, November). *I.G.B.: An educational treatment design for the autism child and adolescent.* Paper presented at the annual conference of the Association for the Severely Handicapped, Denver, Colorado.

Frank Porter Graham Snapshot. (2009, November). *Developing structured work systems for students with ASD.* Available at www.fpg.unc.edu

Hume, K. (2004). "I can do it myself!" Using work systems to build independence in students with autism spectrum disorders. *The Reporter, 10*(1), 4-6, 16. Available at the Indiana Resource Center for Autism, www.iidc.indiana.edu

Hume, K., Boyd, B., McBee, M., Coman, D., Gutierrez, A., Shaw, E., Sperry, L., et al. (2011). Assessing implementation of comprehensive treatment models for young children with ASD: Reliability and validity of two measures. *Research in Autism Spectrum Disorders*, 1–11.

Hume, K., & Carnahan, C. (2008*). Implementation checklist for structured work systems and activity organization.* Chapel Hill, NC: The University of North Carolina, The National Professional Development Center on Autism Spectrum Disorders, Frank Porter Graham Child Development Institute.

Hume, K., & Carnahan, C. (2008). *Steps for implementation: Structured work systems and activity organization.* Chapel Hill, NC: The University of North Carolina, The National Professional Development Center on Autism Spectrum Disorders, Frank Porter Graham Child Development Institute.

Hume, K., Loftin, R., & Lantz, J. (2009). Increasing independence in autism spectrum disorders: A review of three focused interventions. *Journal of Autism and Developmental Disorders, 39*(9), 1329-1338.

Hume, K., & Odom, S. (2007). Effects of an individual work system on the independent functioning of students with autism. *Journal of Autism and Developmental Disorders, 37*(6), 1166-1180.

Hume, K., Plavnick, J., & Odom, S. L. (2012). Promoting task accuracy and independence in students with autism across educational setting through the use of individual work systems. *Journal of Autism and Developmental Disorders.*

MacDuff, G. S., Krantz, P., & McClannahan, L. (1993). Teaching children with autism to use photographic activity schedules: Maintenance and generalization of complex response chains. *Journal of Applied Behavior Analysis, 26*(1), 89-97.

National Professional Development Center on Autism Spectrum Disorders. (2008). *Module: Individualized work systems.* Chapel Hill, NC: The University of North Carolina, The National Professional Development Center on Autism Spectrum Disorders, Frank Porter Graham Child Development Institute.

Ozonoff, S., & Cathcart, K. (1998). Effectiveness of a home program intervention for young children with autism. *Journal of Autism and Developmental Disorders, 28*(1), 25-32.

Panerai, S., Ferrante, L., Caputo, V., & Impellizzeri, C. (1998). Use of structured teaching for treatment of children with autism and severe and profound mental retardation. *Education and Training in Mental Retardation and Developmental Disabilities, 33*(4), 367-374.

Panerai, S., Ferrante, L., & Zingale, M. (2002). Benefits of the treatment and education of autistic and communication handicapped children (TEACCH) programme as compared with a non-specific approach. *Journal of Intellectual Disability Research, 46*(4), 318-327.

Schopler, E., Mesibov, G., & Hearsey, K. (1995). Structured teaching in the TEACCH system. In E. Schopler & G. Mesibov (Eds.)., Learning and cognition in autism (pp. 243-267). New York, NY: Kluwer Academic/Plenum.

Tsang, S. K., Shek, D. T., Lam, L. L., Tang, F. L., & Cheung, P. M. (2006). Brief report: Application of the TEACCH program on Chinese preschool children with autism – Does culture make a difference? *Journal of Autism and Developmental Disorders, 37*(2), 390-396.

# APPENDIX B

## The Assessment of Basic Language and Learning Skills – Revised

Partington, J. (2006). *The assessment of basic language and learning skills* (rev. ed.). Walnut Creek, CA: Behavior Analysis Inc.

**Synopsis:** Skills that can be maintained in structured work systems. The numbering matches the protocol and does not include categories of skills that are not applicable to structured work systems.

### Cooperation and Reinforcer Effectiveness

Task A19. Task completion serves as a reinforcer

### Visual Performance

Task B1. Puzzle with a single piece type of inset

Task B2. Form box

Task B3. Matches identical objects to sample

Task B4. Matches objects to pictures

Task B5. Matches identical pictures to sample

Task B6. Matches pictures to objects

Task B7. Fluent matching

Task B8. Sorts non-identical items

Task B9. Block designs on picture cards

Task B10. Puzzles with multiple connecting pieces in an inset-type frame

Task B11. Puzzles with a square-edged border frame

Task B12. Block designs from picture

Task B13. Sequence pattern to match a visual model

Task B14. Puzzles with multiple pieces that must be juxtaposed

Task B15. Jigsaw puzzles

Task B16. Matches associated pictures

Task B17. Sorts by function

Task B18. Sorts by feature

Task B19. Sorts by class

Task B22. Extends a sequence pattern

Task B23. Replicates simple three-dimensional objects

Task B25. Seriation

Task B26. Picture sequences

Task B27. Mazes

## Requests

Task F9. Requests missing items needed for a task

Task F12. Requests help

## Follow Classroom Routines

Task N2. Works independently on non-academic activities

Task N7. Works independently on academic activities

Task N8. Gets and returns own materials

Task N9. Completes a task and brings work to teacher or puts away materials

## Generalized Responding

Task P1. Generalizes across stimuli

Task P3. Generalizes across environments

## Reading Skills

Task Q5. Matches words with pictures

Task Q6. Matches words to words

Task Q8. Matches individual letters to letters on word cards

Task Q9. Fills in missing letter of words

Task Q14. Fills in missing words

Task Q16. Reads and follows simple instructions on worksheets

Task Q17. Reads passages and answers comprehension questions

## Math Skills

Task R8. Matches number with same amount of objects

Task R14. Adds items to specified quantity

Task R20. Adds numbers

Task R21. Time telling

Task R23. Identifies all coins by value

Item R24. Interchanges coins to arrive at equal value

## Writing Skills

Item S1. Marks on paper

Item S2. Colors between lines

Item S3. Traces lines and shapes

Item S4. Traces letters and numbers

Item S5. Copies straight lines

Item S6. Copies curved lines

Item S7. Copies letters

Item S8. Copies numbers

Item S9. Prints letters

Item S10. Prints numbers

## Spelling

Item T1. Matches individual letters to letters on word card

Item T2. Fills in missing letter of words

Item T3. Copies words

Item T4. Writes in missing letter of words

## Dressing Skills

Item U4. Buttons shirts on and off

Item U8. Unzips zippers

Item U9. Fastens zipper

Item U11. Fastens buttons

Item U12. Uses snaps

Item U13. Uses buckles

Item U15. Ties shoes

## Fine-motor Skills

Item Z1. Marks on paper with a crayon

Item Z2. Places objects in a form box

Item Z4. Multiple puzzle pieces into a frame

Item Z5. Blocks on block design cards

Item Z7. Places pegs in a pegboard

Item Z9. Clothespins on a line

Item Z10. Colors within boundaries

Item Z11. Opens resealable zipper plastic bags

Item Z12. Snips with scissors

Item Z13. Stacks blocks

Item Z14. Strings beads

Item Z15. Removes lids of jars

Item Z16. Cuts across paper with scissors

Item Z20. Roughly copies shapes and patterns

Item Z21. Pastes shapes on outlined picture

Item Z22. Pastes shapes on plain paper picture

Item Z23. Objects on pegs

Item Z24. Replaces lids of jars

Item Z25. Uses pincer grasp

Item Z26. Folds a piece of paper

Item Z27. Cuts out shapes

Item Z28. Accurately copies shapes and patterns

## Brigance Comprehensive Inventory of Basic Skills - Revised

Curriculum Associates, Inc. (1999). *Brigance comprehensive inventory of basic skills – revised*. Woburn, MA: Curriculum Associates, Inc.

**Synopsis:** Skills that can be maintained in structured work systems. The numbering matches the protocol and does not include categories of skills that are not applicable to structured work systems.

## *Readiness*

*Self-Help Skills*

> Item 2. Buttons clothing
> Item 4. Ties shoes

*Draws a Person*

> Item 1. Draws a person with recognizable, distinct body part. Body parts included in picture include numbers 1 through 13: head, legs, ears, feet, arms, shoulders, trunk, eyes, nose, hair, neck, hands, mouth

*Visual Motor Skills – Forms*

> Item 1. Copies forms including numbers 1 through 7: circle, cross, x, square, rectangle, triangle, diamond

*Visual Discrimination – Forms, Letters, and Words*

> Item 1. Visually discriminates which one of four printed symbols is different including numbers 1-20: Forms (1-5), Uppercase Letters (6-10), Lowercase Letters (11-15), Words (16-20)

*Prints Uppercase Letters in Sequence*

> Item 1. Prints letters A through Z

*Prints Lowercase Letters in Sequence*

> Item 1. Prints letters a through z

*Prints Personal Data*

> Item 1. First name
> Item 2. Last name
> Item 3. Age
> Item 4. Telephone number
> Item 5. Middle name
> Item 6. Address

*Counts Objects*

    Item 1. Counts a group of objects with quantities to 3, 6, 8, 12, 16, 24

*Joins Sets*

    Item 1. Joins groups of like objects with sums to 3, 4, 5, 6, 7, 8, 9, 10

*Numeral Comprehension*

    Item 1. Shows quantities to match symbols 1, 2, 3, 4, 5, 6, 7, 8, 9, 10

*Writes Numerals in Sequence*

    Item 1. Writes numerals in sequence from memory to 3, 4, 5, 6, 7, 8, 9, 10, 11-20, 21-30, 31-40, 41-50, 51-60, 61-70, 71-80, 81-90, 91-100

## Word Analysis

*Divides Words Into Syllables*

    Item 1. One vowel sound

    Item 2. Like consonants between vowels

    Item 3. Unlike consonants between vowels

    Item 4. Consonant blends and digraphs between two vowels

    Item 5. One consonant between two vowels

    Item 6. Suffixes

    Item 7. Three vowel sounds

    Item 8. Ending le

    Item 9. Prefixes

## Spelling

*Spells Number Words*

    Items 1 through 38

## Writing

*Writes Cursive Lowercase Letters in Sequence*

    Item 1. a through z

*Writes Uppercase Letters in Sequence*

    Item 1. A through Z

*Writes Personal Data*

    Items 1-13: Name; age; date of birth; address; telephone; school; grade; teacher; room; parents or guardians; in case of emergency, contact; name of family physician; signature

*Addresses Envelope*

    Item 1. Addresses an envelope with numbers 1 through 8

## Reference Skills

*Identifies Following and Preceding Letters of the Alphabet*

    Item 1. Identifies letters that follow

    Item 2. Identifies letters that precede

*Alphabetizes Words*

    Item 1. Alphabetizes words with consecutive first letters; non-consecutive first letters; the same first letter; the same first two letters; the same first three letters; the same first four letters

*Outlining*

    Item 1. Reads a passage and outlines by: topic, subtopic, details

*Uses Dictionary*

    Item 1. Uses dictionary to complete 1-12

*Uses Scale and Legend on a Map*

    Item 1. Uses scale to determine distances

    Item 2. Uses legend to determine regional information

*Uses Special Purpose Maps*

    Item 1. Uses legend to identify regions

    Item 2. Uses direction to identify regions

    Item 3. Uses latitude and longitude to find locations

    Item 4. Uses scale to find distances

    Item 5. Combines information from two maps

    Item 6. Infers information

## Numbers

*Arranges Numbers in Order*

    Item 1. Writes numbers in numerical order for at least one of two lists for quantities: 1 to 10; 10 to 100; 100 to 1000; 10 to 10,000

*Reads Meters and Gauges*

    Item 1. Reads meters and gauges with graduations of: one, two, five, ten, twenty-five

*Rounds Numbers*

    Item 1. Rounds numbers to the nearest: ten, hundred, thousand, ten thousand, tenth, hundredth, thousandth, millionth

## Number Facts

*Addition Facts*

    Item 1. Knows facts for sums up to: 6, 8, 10, 12, 14, 16, 19

*Subtraction Facts*

    Item 1. Knows differences for minuends up to: 6, 8, 10, 12, 14, 16, 19

*Multiplication facts*

    Item 1. Knows products for multipliers up to: 2, 3, 4, 5, 6, 7, 8, 9

*Division Facts*

    Item 1. Knows quotients for divisors up to: 2, 3, 4, 5, 6, 7, 8, 9

### Computation of Whole Numbers

*Addition of Whole Numbers*

    Item 1. Adds whole numbers with 2 digits without regrouping

    Item 2. Adds whole numbers with 2 digits with 1 regrouping

    Item 3. Adds whole numbers with 3 digits without regrouping

    Item 4. Adds whole numbers with 3 digits with 1 regrouping

    Item 5. Adds whole numbers with 3 digits with 2 regroupings

    Item 6. Adds whole numbers with 4 digits with 3 regroupings

*Subtraction of Whole Numbers*

    Item 1. Subtracts whole numbers with 2 digits without regrouping

    Item 2. Subtracts whole numbers with 2 digits with 1 regrouping

    Item 3. Subtracts whole numbers with 3 digits without regrouping

    Item 4. Subtracts whole numbers with 3 digits with 1 regrouping

    Item 5. Subtracts whole numbers with 3 digits with 2 regroupings

    Item 6. Subtracts whole numbers with 4 digits with 3 regroupings

*Multiplication of Whole Numbers*

    Item 1. Multiplies whole numbers with 2 digits x 1 digit without regrouping

    Item 2. Multiplies whole numbers with 2 digits x 1 digit with regrouping

    Item 3. Multiplies whole numbers with 3 digits x 2 digits with regrouping and no zero in multiplier

    Item 4. Multiplies whole numbers with 3 digits x 2 digits with regrouping and zero in multiplier

    Item 5. Multiplies whole numbers with 3 digits x 3 digits with regrouping and no zero in multiplier

    Item 6. Multiplies whole numbers with 3 digits x 3 digits with regrouping and zero in multiplier

*Division of Whole Numbers*

Item 1. Divides whole numbers with 2 digits by 1 digit

Item 2. Divides whole numbers with 2 digits by 2 digits

Item 3. Divides whole numbers with 3 digits by 2 digits with 1 digit in quotient

Item 4. Divides whole numbers with 3 digits by 2 digits with 2 digits in quotient

Item 5. Divides whole numbers with 4 digits by 3 digits with no zero in quotient

Item 6. Divides whole numbers with 4 digits by 3 digits with zero in quotient

## Fractions and Mixed Numbers

*Addition of Fractions and Mixed Numbers*

Item 1. Addition of fractions and mixed numbers

Item 2. Subtraction of fractions and mixed numbers

Item 3. Multiplication of fractions and mixed numbers

Item 4. Division of fractions and mixed numbers

## Decimals

*Writes Decimals in Order of Value*

Item 1. Tenths

Item 2. Tenths and hundredths

Item 3. Tenths, hundredths, and thousandths

*Addition of Decimals*

*Subtraction of Decimals*

*Multiplication of Decimals*

*Division of Decimals*

## Percents

*Converts Fractions to Percents*

*Converts Fractions to Percents II*

*Converts Decimals to Percents*

## Time

*Tells Time*

*Equivalent Units of Time*

*Converts Units of Time*

*Equivalent Calendar Units*

*Converts Calendar Units*

*Uses a Calendar*

## *Money*

*Recognizes Money*

*Equivalent Values of Coins and the Dollar Bill*

*Totals Values of Groups of Coins*

*Converts Coins*

*Makes Change*

## *U.S. Customary Measurement and Geometry*

*Equivalent U.S. Customary Linear Measures*

*Measures With Inch Ruler*

*Converts U.S. Customary Linear Measurements*

*Converts U.S. Customary Liquid Measurements*

*Converts U.S. Customary Weight Measurements*

*Understands Basic Geometric Shapes And Concepts*

## *Metrics*

*Understands Equivalent Metric Measurements*

*Converts Linear Metric Measurements*

*Converts Volume And Mass Metric Measurements*

*Measures With Metric Ruler*

## Brigance Diagnostic Inventory of Early Development II

Curriculum Associates, Inc. (1991). *Brigance diagnostic inventory of early development II*. Woburn, MA: Curriculum Associates, Inc.

**Synopsis:** Skills that can be maintained in structured work systems. The numbering used matches the protocol and does not include categories of skills that are not applicable to structured work systems.

### *C. Fine-Motor Skills and Behaviors*

*General Eye/Finger/Hand/Manipulative Skills*

Item 32. Puts objects such as blocks into a container, using good grasp and voluntary release

Item 36. Holds container with one hand and releases objects into it with the other hand

Item 38. "Nests" or stacks objects graduated in size

Item 44. Folds paper in half; may be imprecise

Item 45. Sorts dissimilar objects

Item 46. Puts a paper clip on paper

Item 48. Folds paper diagonally and creases it

Item 49. Prints first name

*Block Tower Building*

Items 2 through 12. Builds a two- to-12-block tower

*Pre-handwriting*

Item 2. Scribbles with crayon, sometimes loses contact with the paper

Item 3. Scribbles with crayon, seldom loses contact with the paper

Item 7. Draws, names, and describes recognizable picture

Item 8. Traces easier uppercase letters such as H, A, T

Item 9. Copies easier uppercase letters such as H, A, T

Item 10. Copies first name

Item 11. Prints first name

Item 12. Colors within lines

Item 14. Traces more difficult lowercase letters

Item 15. Copies more difficult lowercase letters

*Draw a Person*

Items 1 through 13. Body parts included in picture: head, legs, ears, arms, trunk, eyes, nose, neck, hands, mouth, shoulders, feet, hair

*Forms*

Items 1 through 9. Copies vertical line, horizontal line, circle, cross, X, square, rectangle, triangle, diamond

*Cutting With Scissors*

Item 3. Snips or makes small cuts in paper

Item 5. Cuts a piece of paper 5 inches

Item 6. Cuts a 5-inch line within ½ inch limits

Item 7. Cuts a triangle with 2-inch sides within ½-inch limits

Item 9. Cuts a 5-inch circle within ½-inch limits

Item 10. Cuts a 5-inch circle within ½-inch limits

Item 11. Cuts a 5-inch curving line within ¼-inch limits

Item 12. Cuts out items such as paper dolls or pictures of animals

*Fastening*

Item 1. Buttons large buttons

Item 2. Snaps front snaps

Item 3. Zips front non-separating zipper

Item 5. Buttons small front buttons

Item 11. Ties shoes

## F. General Knowledge and Comprehension

*Body Parts – Receptive*

Items 1 through 29. Eyes, nose, mouth, hair, feet, ears, tongue, head, legs, arms, fingers, teeth, thumbs, toes, neck, stomach, chest, back, knees, chin, fingernails, heels, ankles, jaw, shoulders, elbows, hips, wrists, waist

*Colors*

Item 3. Matches red, blue, green, yellow, orange, purple, brown, black, pink, gray, white

*Shape Concepts*

Item 1. Matches circle, square, triangle, rectangle, diamond

*Quantitative Concepts*

Item 1. Big/little

Item 3. Full/empty

Item 4. Heavy/light

Item 5. Tall/short

Item 6. Fat/thin

Item 7. Fast/slow

Item 8. All/none

Item 9. Long/short

Item 10. Large/small

Item 11. Deep/shallow

Item 12. Thick/thin

Item 13. Wide/narrow

Item 16. Huge/tiny

*Directional/Positional Concepts*

Item 1. Close/open

Item 2. Front/back

Item 3. In/out

Item 4. Behind/in front of

Item 5. Bottom/top

Item 6. Over/under

Item 7. Up/down

Item 8. Forward/backward

Item 9. Away from/toward

Item 10. Low/high

Item 11. Above/below

Item 12. Center/corner

Item 13. Right/left

Item 14. Right/left of others

*Classifying*

Items 1 through 16. Animals, toys, means of travel or things to ride in, clothes, foods, dishes, people, pets, numbers, things to read, fruits, vegetables, tools, furniture, shapes, musical instruments

## G. Social and Emotional Development

*Play Skills and Behaviors*

Item 8. Plays with a variety of toys, doing different activities with each

*Initiative and Engagement Skills and Behaviors*

Item 18. Engages in activities for 5 minutes

Item 19. Engages in activities for 10 minutes

Item 20. Engages in activities for 15 minutes

Item 21. Engages in activities for 20 minutes or more

Item 26. Usually remains at a 10-to-12 minute task until it is time to quit or change

Item 30. Remains engaged in an assigned task even when minor distractions are present

## H. Readiness

*Visual Discrimination – Forms and Uppercase Letters*

Items 1 through 10. Visually discriminates which one of four printed symbols is different. See protocol for forms. Uppercase letters O, I, P, V, X

*Visual Discrimination – Lowercase Letters and Words*

Items 1 through 10. Visually discriminates which one of four printed symbols is different. o, c, e, b, n, on, be, can, they, was

*Uppercase Letters*

Item 1. A through Z

*Lowercase Letters*

Item 1. a through z

## I. Basic Reading Skills

*Reads Color Words*

Item 1. Reads red, blue, green, yellow, orange, purple, brown, black, pink, gray, white

*Reads Number Words*

Item 1. Reads one, four, two, three, six, ten, five, nine, seven, eight

## J. Manuscript Writing

*Prints Personal Data*

Items 1 through 8. Prints first letter of first name, nickname, real name, last name, age, telephone number, middle name, address

*Prints Uppercase Letters In Sequence*

Item 1. A through Z

*Prints Lowercase Letters in Sequence*

Item 1. a through z

*Prints Simple Sentences*

    Item 1. One through four sentences

## K. Basic Math

*Number Concepts*

    Item 3. Counts objects 1 through 10

*Numeral Comprehension*

    Item 1. Matches quantity with symbol 1 through 10

*Numerals in Sequence*

    Item 1. Writes numerals in sequence from memory to: 3, 5, 10, 20, 30, 40, 50, 60, 70, 80, 90, 100

*Writes Following and Preceding Numerals*

    Item 1. Writes numeral that follows a given numeral: 2, 3, 1, 4, 5, 8, 10, 9, 7, 12, 11

    Item 2. Writes numeral that precedes a given numeral: 2, 3, 1, 4, 6, 5, 8, 10, 9, 7, 12, 11

*Addition Combinations*

    Item 1. Knows addition facts with sums to 4, 6, 8, 10, 12, 14, 16, 18

*Subtraction Combinations*

    Item 1. Knows subtraction facts with minuends to 4, 6, 8, 10

*Recognition of Money*

    Item 2. Gives monetary value of United States coins and a dollar bill: one cent, five cents, ten cents, twenty-five cents, one hundred cents

*Time*

    Item 8. Tells time to the hour

    Item 9. Tells time to the half-hour

    Item 10. Tells time to the quarter-hour

## HELP Strands 0 to Three Years

Parks, S. (1995). *Hawaii early learning profile (0-3 years) assessment strands*. Palo Alto, CA: VORT Corporation.

**Synopsis:** Skills that can be maintained in structured work systems. The numbering matches the protocol and does not include categories of skills that are not applicable to structured work systems.

### *Fine-Motor*

*Development of Voluntary Release*

      Item 4.56. Puts objects in container

      Item 4.60. Puts three or more objects into small container

      Item 4.67. Puts many objects into container without removing any

      Item 4.84. Puts tiny objects into small container

*Bilateral and Midline Skills*

      Item 4.38. Transfers object

      Item 1.61. Unwraps a toy

### *Perceptual-Motor Integration of Foundations of Fine-Motor*

*Prewriting*

      Item 4.65. Scribbles spontaneously

      Item 4.83. Makes first designs or spontaneous forms

      Item 4.86. Copies a circle

*Block Construction*

      Item 4.61. Builds tower using two cubes

      Item 4.69. Builds tower using three cubes

      Item 4.72. Builds tower using four cubes

      Item 4.77. Builds tower using six cubes

      Item 4.87. Builds tower using eight cubes

      Item 4.92. Builds tower using nine cubes

*Formboard*

      Item 1.57. Removes round piece from formboard

      Item 1.63. Places cylinders in matching hole in container

Item 1.72. Places round piece in formboard

Item 1.86. Places square piece in formboard

Item 1.114. Places triangular piece in formboard

*Paper Activities*

Item 4.85. Folds paper in half

*Pegboard*

Item 4.47. Removes pegs from pegboard

Item 4.62. Places one round peg in pegboard

Item 4.70. Places six round pegs in pegboard

Item 4.90. Places six square pegs in pegboard

*Stringing Beads*

Item 4.74. Strings one 1-inch bead

Item 4.80. Strings three 1-inch beads

Item 4.93. Strings ½-inch beads (Cheerios)

*Scissors*

Item 4.81. Snips with scissors

Item 4.88. Snips on line using scissors

## Cognitive

*Spatial Relationships*

Item 4.48. Takes objects out of container

Item 1.58. Takes ring stack apart

Item 4.60. Puts three or more objects into container

Item 4.61. Builds tower using two cubes

Item 1.64. Stacks rings

Item 1.147. Completes three to four piece puzzle

*Concepts (Pictures)*

Item 1.107. Matches objects to pictures

*Discrimination/Classification (Matching and Sorting)*

Item 1.85. Matches objects

Item 1.108. Sorts objects

Item 1.136. Matches shapes (circle, triangle, square)

Item 1.137. Matches colors (black, white)

Item 1.139. Matches identical simple pictures of objects

Item 1.144. Matches primary colors (blue, red, yellow)

Item 1.145. Matches similar pictures of objects

Item 1.146. Sorts shapes (circle, square, triangle)

Item 1.156. Sorts colors (3 different)

*Discrimination/Classification (Size)*

Item 1.70. Shows understanding of size

Item 1.72. Nests two, then three cans

Item 1.109. Assembles four nesting blocks

Item 1.148. Stacks rings in correct order

*Discrimination/Classification (Associative)*

Item 1.126. Identifies clothing items for different occasions

## HELP for Preschoolers: Assessment Strands: Ages 3-6 Years

Parks, S. (1995). *Hawaii early learning profile (3-6 years) assessment strands*. Palo Alto, CA: VORT Corporation.

**Synopsis:** Skills that can be maintained in structured work systems. The numbering matches the protocol and does not include categories of skills that are not applicable to structured work systems.

### *Cognitive*

*Problem Solving/Reasoning*

       Item 1.165. Locates pictured analogy

       Item 1.183. Tells a word that associates with another word

       Item 1.190. Places illustration in correct sequence

       Item 1.191. Puts manipulative shapes together to form same design as illustrated model

       Item 1.285. Groups objects by at least two analogies

*Discrimination/Classification: Matching and Sorting*

       Item 1.196. Matches like items based on appearance

       Item 1.197. Matches like items based on function

       Item 1.202. Locates which out of 5 objects or pictures does not belong in same class/category

       Item 1.203. Places 3 pictures in sequence

       Item 1.204. Matches like items based on category

       Item 1.236. Places 4 pictures in sequence

*Discrimination/Classification: Size*

       Item 1.233. Sorts 5 multiple-classed objects or pictured objects according to class/category

       Item 1.238. Sorts items by category

       Item 1.243. Sorts items by appearance

       Item 1.244. Sorts items by function

*Discrimination/Classification: Associative*

       Item 1.265. Finds the incongruous/out-of-place/misdirected object

       Item 1.272. Identifies an object that does not belong to a group based on one or more characteristics

       Item 1.281. Compares items by appearance (size, color, designs, parts)

       Item 1.282. Compares items by category and function

       Item 1.283. Groups objects by two analogies

*Attention*

    Item 1.187. Attends to task without supervision

    Item 1.189. Remains on task when distractions are present

    Item 1.217. Starts task with no reminding or prompting

    Item 1.218. Attends to task without supervision for 10 minutes

    Item 1.219. Remains on task for 5 to 10 minutes when distractions are present

    Item 1.250. Completes task with little prompting

    Item 1.280. Attends to task without supervision for 15 minutes

*Reading Readiness*

    Item 1.206. Points to pictures that represent sequence of events in a story

    Item 1.258. Matches identical letters in group of different letters

    Item 1.259. Matches words in group of words

    Item 1.288. Fills in a word when read a passage with words missing

    Item 1.297. Answers literal comprehension questions about stories read

    Item 1.298. Answers interpretative comprehension questions about a story read

*Math Readiness*

    Item 1.174. Identifies and counts quantities of one, two, three, or four

    Item 1.175. Locates big and little objects in groups of 2

    Item 1.192. Sorts according to shape, size, and length

    Item 1.195. Determines which of 2 groups has more and less, many and few

    Item 1.212. Names penny, nickel, quarter, and dime

    Item 1.214. Constructs set of objects

    Item 1.215. Locates first, middle, and last in group of objects

    Item 1.216. Matches coins

    Item 1.222. Selects long, longer, and longest from group of objects

    Item 1.235. Identifies and counts quantities of at least 6

    Item 1.237. Locates big, bigger, and biggest, and small, smaller, and smallest in group of objects

    Item 1.248. Locates object of given number in group of 10

    Item 1.249. Matches groups having equal numbers of objects up to 10

    Item 1.256. Arranges objects in order of size from smallest to largest

    Item 1.274. Reads hour and half-hour time

    Item 1.275. Matches time with daily activities

    Item 1.278. Reads numerals on clock face and associates time with routine activity

    Item 1.290. Identifies what number comes before and after a given number, or between 2 numbers

    Item 1.301. Reads and writes numerals to 49

*Writing Skills*

    Item 1.200. Colors within the lines of a circle

    Item 1.207. Draws a geometric design from a pattern

    Item 1.213. Traces own name

    Item 1.220. Draws line between 2 parallel lines

    Item 1.241. Draws recognizable face with eyes, nose, mouth

    Item 1.255. Prints own first or last name, copying model

    Item 1.260. Prints letters and numbers, copying model

    Item 1.268. Prints simple words, copying models

    Item 1.269. Colors within heavy outlines/within faint outlines

    Item 1.270. Prints own first name without a model

    Item 1.271. Prints numbers and letters without a model

    Item 1.294. Prints all letters of alphabet, all numbers 0-9 correctly without models

    Item 1.295. Prints simple words without model

## Language

*Receptive Language: Understanding Words*

    Item 1.228. Sequences a 3-picture story that has been read

    Item 2.144. Identifies words that rhyme

## Fine-Motor

*Prewriting*

    Item 4.101. Places small pegs in holes on board

    Item 4.107. Draws a square following a model

    Item 4.109. Matches 6 or more colors

    Item 4.111. Completes a picture of a stick person

    Item 4.114. Draws a diagonal line and a zigzag line following models

    Item 4.121. Makes fine visual discriminations, matches letters that look very similar

    Item 4.122. Draws a picture of at least three objects

    Item 4.125. Identifies look-alike words correctly

*Blocks/Puzzles*

    Item 4.94. Puts together simple puzzles

    Item 4.95. Makes a bridge with 3 blocks

    Item 4.97. Builds tower of more than 9 blocks without assistance

    Item 4.102. Reproduces a two-dimensional block design-after demonstration

Item 4.124. Puts together complex/interlocking puzzle

Item 4.126. Builds 5-block bridge

*Stringing Beads*

Item 4.98. Strings small beads, cubes, cylinders based on a simple shape pattern

Item 4.112. Strings small beads reproducing color and shape sequence/pattern

*Scissors*

Item 4.96. Cuts across paper following curved line/circle

Item 4.113. Cuts out small square/triangle with scissors

Item 4.119. Cuts out picture following general shape

Item 4.120. Cuts cloth/other material with scissors

Item 4.123. Cuts out complex pictures following outline

## Social

*Responsibility/Rules*

Item 5.130. Sits without moving when involved in an activity

Item 5.140. Performs assigned task

Item 5.209. Displays behavior appropriate for the situation/place

Item 5.220. Plays and works without disrupting work of others

*Social Interactions and Play*

Item 5.111. Remains calm if goals cannot be reached

Item 5.113. Shows independence from adult

Item 5.114. Asks for assistance when needed

Item 5.116. Demonstrates respect for property

Item 5.214. Maintains silence when appropriate

## Self-Help

*Dressing*

Item 6.127. Closes 2 of 3 front snaps

Item 6.151. Buttons front-opening clothing

Item 6.166. Zips up front-opening clothing

Item 6.193. Ties laces into a bow knot

*Undressing*

Item 6.96. Unzips and unsnaps clothing

Item 6.133. Unbuttons clothing

Item 6.172. Opens all fasteners

## The Star Program: Strategies for Teaching Based on Autism Research

Arick, J., Loos, L., Falco, R., & Krug, D. (2003). *The STAR program: Strategies for teaching based on autism research*. Austin, TX: PRO-ED.

**Synopsis:** Skills that can be maintained in structured work systems. The numbering matches the protocol and does not include categories of skills that are not applicable to structured work systems.

### Level One

*Receptive Language*

   Item 7. Matching: Object to object

   Item 8. Matching: Picture to picture

   Item 9. Matching: Object to picture

   Item 11. Labels of objects

   Item 12. Labels of pictures

   Item 13. Identification of body parts

*Preacademic Concepts*

   Item 2. Matching colors

   Item 3. Matching shapes

   Item 4. Coloring/scribbling

*Play and Social Interaction Concepts*

   Item 2. Playing with toys: Constructive and Functional

   Item 3. Independent play

### Level Two

*Receptive Language Concepts*

   Item 1. Expanded labels

   Item 2. Accelerated labels

   Item 3. Identification of people

   Item 4. Actions: Pictures

   Item 5. Actions: Two-step commands

   Item 6. Locations and commands

   Item 7. Sorting categories

   Item 8. Picture sequencing

*Functional Routines*

    Item 8. Independent work

*Preacademic Concepts*

    Item 2. Math: Counting 1 to 10 objects

    Item 3. Math: Receptive identification of numbers 1 to 10

    Item 5. Math: Receptive counting sets of objects

    Item 6. Math: Matching sets of objects with numbers 1 to 10

    Item 10. Reading: Receptive identification of first name, match to picture

    Item 11. Reading: Sight word reading and match to picture

    Item 12. Writing: Tracing name, letters, and numbers

    Item 13. Writing: Coloring within lines and attention to task

    Item 14. Other: Cutting and pasting

*Play and Social Interaction Concepts*

    Item 2. Playing with toys and independent constructive play

## Level Three

*Receptive Language Concepts*

    Item 1. Functions of objects and community members

    Item 2. Prepositions

    Item 3. Descriptors

    Item 4. Opposites

    Item 5. Gender identification

    Item 6. Possessives

    Item 7. First, next, last

*Functional Routines*

    Item 9. Academic seatwork

*Preacademic Concepts*

    Item 2. Math: Receptive identification of numbers

    Item 4. Math: Counting objects using numbers

    Item 5. Math: Adding one-digit numbers

    Item 6. Math: Subtracting one-digit numbers

    Item 7. Math: Identification of money

    Item 8. Math: Time telling

Item 11. Reading: Identification of first and last names

Item 12. Reading: Sight words

Item 13. Reading: Reading a simple book

Item 14. Writing: Tracing and copying words

Item 16. Writing: Writing from memory

Item 17. Other: Coloring, cutting, and pasting

*Play and Social Interaction Concepts*

Item 1. Functional play

# APPENDIX C

Blank Data Sheets and Forms

# Skill Acquisition Program

*INDEPENDENT WORK TASK ANALYSIS DATA SHEET*

| SKILL: Work Basket System | STUDENT'S NAME: |
| --- | --- |
| AREA: Cognitive/Learning | TARGET BEHAVIOR: Student will complete a set of work baskets when given the Sd. |
| Sd: "Do your work," "work time" or "basket time" | PREREQUISITES: Student can perform tasks in baskets independently. |
| PRIMARY INSTRUCTOR: | PROCEDURAL STEPS: Student is prompted through basket activities with trainer using prompts. Prompts are gradually faded out. |

| DATE: | | | | | | | | |
| --- | --- | --- | --- | --- | --- | --- | --- | --- |
| TIME: | | | | | | | | |
| PROMPTS: | | | | | | | | |
| DURATION: | | | | | | | | |
| BASKET ITEMS: | | | | | | | | |
| 29. Occupies time appropriately after completing baskets. | 29 | 29 | 29 | 29 | 29 | 29 | 29 | 29 |
| 28. Asks for help if materials are missing. | 28 | 28 | 28 | 28 | 28 | 28 | 28 | 28 |
| 27. Accesses reinforcer. | 27 | 27 | 27 | 27 | 27 | 27 | 27 | 27 |
| 26. Puts completed basket into "finished" basket or area. | 26 | 26 | 26 | 26 | 26 | 26 | 26 | 26 |
| 25. Puts activity back into basket. | 25 | 25 | 25 | 25 | 25 | 25 | 25 | 25 |
| 24. Completes activity. | 24 | 24 | 24 | 24 | 24 | 24 | 24 | 24 |
| 23. Sets up activity. | 23 | 23 | 23 | 23 | 23 | 23 | 23 | 23 |
| 22. Takes activity out of basket. | 22 | 22 | 22 | 22 | 22 | 22 | 22 | 22 |
| 21. Places third basket in front of self. | 21 | 21 | 21 | 21 | 21 | 21 | 21 | 21 |
| 20. Matches third shape. | 20 | 20 | 20 | 20 | 20 | 20 | 20 | 20 |
| 19. Pulls off third shape. | 19 | 19 | 19 | 19 | 19 | 19 | 19 | 19 |
| 18. Puts completed basket into "finished" basket or area. | 18 | 18 | 18 | 18 | 18 | 18 | 18 | 18 |
| 17. Puts activity back into basket. | 17 | 17 | 17 | 17 | 17 | 17 | 17 | 17 |
| 16. Completes activity. | 16 | 16 | 16 | 16 | 16 | 16 | 16 | 16 |
| 15. Sets up activity. | 15 | 15 | 15 | 15 | 15 | 15 | 15 | 15 |
| 14. Takes activity out of basket. | 14 | 14 | 14 | 14 | 14 | 14 | 14 | 14 |
| 13. Places second basket in front of self. | 13 | 13 | 13 | 13 | 13 | 13 | 13 | 13 |
| 12. Matches second shape. | 12 | 12 | 12 | 12 | 12 | 12 | 12 | 12 |
| 11. Pulls off second shape. | 11 | 11 | 11 | 11 | 11 | 11 | 11 | 11 |
| 10. Puts completed basket into "finished" basket or area. | 10 | 10 | 10 | 10 | 10 | 10 | 10 | 10 |
| 9. Puts activity back into basket. | 9 | 9 | 9 | 9 | 9 | 9 | 9 | 9 |
| 8. Completes activity. | 8 | 8 | 8 | 8 | 8 | 8 | 8 | 8 |
| 7. Sets up activity. | 7 | 7 | 7 | 7 | 7 | 7 | 7 | 7 |
| 6. Takes activity out of basket. | 6 | 6 | 6 | 6 | 6 | 6 | 6 | 6 |
| 5. Places first basket in front of self. | 5 | 5 | 5 | 5 | 5 | 5 | 5 | 5 |
| 4. Matches first shape. | 4 | 4 | 4 | 4 | 4 | 4 | 4 | 4 |
| 3. Pulls off first shape. | 3 | 3 | 3 | 3 | 3 | 3 | 3 | 3 |
| 2. Sits in chair. | 2 | 2 | 2 | 2 | 2 | 2 | 2 | 2 |
| 1. Walks to basket area. | 1 | 1 | 1 | 1 | 1 | 1 | 1 | 1 |
| STAFF INITIALS: | | | | | | | | |
| LEVEL OF MASTERY: | | | | | | | | |

| Scoring Code: | Prompts | Comments/Observations: |
| --- | --- | --- |
| / Correct | P-Physical | |
| - Prompted | G-Gestural | __/__/_____ |
| X Incorrect | S-Visual | |
| O Circle total | V-Verbal prompt from a distance | __/__/_____ |
| correct | 0-Does not perform step | __/__/_____ |

| Criterion for Mastery: | Basket Items: | C. | F. | I. |
| --- | --- | --- | --- | --- |
| | A. | D. | G. | J. |
| | B. | E. | H. | K. |

**158**

## Work System Data Sheet (adapted from TEACCH)

**Worker's Name:** _____ **Date:** _____ **Work System:** _____

### Information Provided

_____ What work?    _____ How much work?    _____ When finished?    _____ What next?

| Task #1 | Checks Schedule | Begins Task | Completes Task | Puts in Finished area |
|---------|-----------------|-------------|----------------|-----------------------|
|         | Independent | Independent | Independent | Independent |
|         | Visual | Visual | Visual | Visual |
|         | Gestural | Gestural | Gestural | Gestural |
|         | Physical | Physical | Physical | Physical |
|         | 0 | 0 | 0 | 0 |

| Task #2 | Checks Schedule | Begins Task | Completes Task | Puts in Finished area |
|---------|-----------------|-------------|----------------|-----------------------|
|         | Independent | Independent | Independent | Independent |
|         | Visual | Visual | Visual | Visual |
|         | Gestural | Gestural | Gestural | Gestural |
|         | Physical | Physical | Physical | Physical |
|         | 0 | 0 | 0 | 0 |

| Task #3 | Checks Schedule | Begins Task | Completes Task | Puts in Finished area |
|---------|-----------------|-------------|----------------|-----------------------|
|         | Independent | Independent | Independent | Independent |
|         | Visual | Visual | Visual | Visual |
|         | Gestural | Gestural | Gestural | Gestural |
|         | Physical | Physical | Physical | Physical |
|         | 0 | 0 | 0 | 0 |

| Task #4 | Checks Schedule | Begins Task | Completes Task | Puts in Finished area |
|---------|-----------------|-------------|----------------|-----------------------|
|         | Independent | Independent | Independent | Independent |
|         | Visual | Visual | Visual | Visual |
|         | Gestural | Gestural | Gestural | Gestural |
|         | Physical | Physical | Physical | Physical |
|         | 0 | 0 | 0 | 0 |

Adapted with permission from Susan Boswell, TEACCH Autism Program. Copyright 2011.

## Structured Work Systems Data Sheet

Worker's Name: _____ Date: _____

Instructor: _____

## System Design

| Tasks | Matching<br>Sorting<br>Assembly/disassembly<br>Packaging<br>Sequencing<br>Office<br>Pre/func academics | Jigs<br>Model<br>Picture dictionary<br>Picture/written directions | |
|---|---|---|---|
| Work System | Number of tasks __3__<br><br>Work period <u>30 minutes</u><br><u>2</u> work periods/day | Tasks on work surface<br>Tasks next to work area<br>Tasks in separate area<br>"Finished" basket<br>"Finished" area | No system<br>Match color, shape, object,<br>numbers, letters<br>List color, shape, object,<br>numbers, letters |
| Environment | Enclosed cubby<br>At desk<br>Common area | Self-contained class<br>Regular education<br>Vocational Lab | |
| What Comes Next | Reinforcer at work area<br>Token<br>Choice time<br>Check schedule<br>Activity at work area | | |

## Data for the Week of _____

| Monday | Tuesday | Wednesday | Thursday | Friday |
|---|---|---|---|---|
| Independent | Independent | Independent | Independent | Independent |
| Visual Cue | Visual Cue | Visual Cue | Visual Cue | Visual Cue |
| Gestural Prompt | Gestural Prompt | Gestural Prompt | Gestural Prompt | Gestural Prompt |
| Physical Prompt | Physical Prompt | Physical Prompt | Physical Prompt | Physical Prompt |
| Verbal Prompt<br>(Last Resort) | Verbal Prompt<br>(Last Resort) | Verbal Prompt<br>(Last Resort) | Verbal Prompt<br>(Last Resort) | Verbal Prompt<br>(Last Resort) |

## Structured Teaching
## Competency-Based Checklist

| Instructor: | Date: |
|---|---|
| Observer: | Length of Observation: |
| Student(s): | Skill/Activity Observed: |

Check off presence of the skill in yes/no boxes. Check N/A if a given skill does not apply within this observation.

| Skills | Yes | No | N/A | Comments |
|---|---|---|---|---|
| The system tells the worker how much work needs to be done. | | | | |
| The system tells the worker what work needs to be done. | | | | |
| The system lets the worker know when he or she is finished. | | | | |
| The system provides information about what happens next. | | | | |
| All work tasks contained in the system are previously mastered. | | | | |
| Work is individualized to the worker's functioning level. | | | | |
| Instructor reserves praise and reinforcement for completion of the system. | | | | |
| Completed tasks are placed in the "finished" area without being taken apart. | | | | |
| Instructors do not reset the work in front of the worker. | | | | |
| Instructors use only nonverbal prompts to teach the system. | | | | |
| Instructor uses the least amount of assistance necessary to help the worker master the system. | | | | |
| Instructor fades physical proximity to the area as the worker gains independence. | | | | |
| Data are collected accurately on a regular schedule. | | | | |
| Data are reviewed regularly and the tasks and system are modified based on that analysis. | | | | |

## Structured Work Assignment Planning Form

| Worker's Name | Task One | Task Two | Task Three |
|---|---|---|---|
| | | | |
| | | | |
| | | | |
| | | | |
| | | | |
| | | | |
| | | | |
| | | | |
| | | | |
| | | | |

## Also by Chris Reeve and Sue Kabot

### Setting up Classroom Spaces That Support Students With Autism Spectrum Disorders

Using clear descriptions and lots of photos, this book shows how to determine what type of furniture and materials to choose for various types of classrooms and how to arrange them in a way that creates an effective learning environment while reducing anxiety and preventing problem behaviors. It uses evidence-based practices of structure and visual supports to enhance the well-being and success of students with ASD. Examples are given for a variety of ages with lots of lists and helpful resources, making this book a must-have resource.

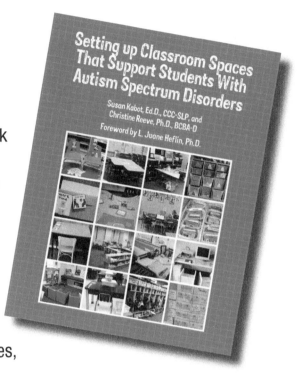

ISBN 9781934575680

**Susan Kabot, EdD, CCC-SLP, and Christine Reeve, PhD, BCBA-D**

**Code 9046**          **Price $23.95**

P.O. Box 23173
Shawnee Mission, Kansas 66283-0173
www.aapcpublishing.net

Lightning Source UK Ltd.
Milton Keynes UK
UKOW07f0837031215

264018UK00010B/32/P